The Case of Ireland Stated

Robert Holmes

THE

CASE OF IRELAND

STATED.

BY

ROBERT HOLMES, ESQ.

"The liberty of man in society is, to be under no other legislative power but that established by consent in the commonwealth, nor under the dominion of any will, or restraint of any law, but what that legislative power shall enact according to the trust put in it."

LOCKE.

Second Edition, corrected.

DUBLIN :

JAMES McGLASHAN, 21, D'OLIER-STREET.

JAMES RIDGWAY, PICCADILLY, LONDON.

MDCCCXLVII.

Dublin : Printed by EDWARD BULL, 6, Bachelor's-walk.

PREFACE.

———•———

WHILE the calamity in the failure of the potato crop of the last year, by which Ireland is afflicted, engages the sympathies and alarms the fears of every class, every sect, and every party in the country—while the physical cause of the disaster has been explored in vain, and inquiries have been made upon the subject, to which no sufficient answer has been given—it is impossible that other inquiries must not, at such a time, and under such circumstances, be forced upon the mind—inquiries deeply interesting, but more capable of solution, and to which more satisfactory replies may be returned. It may be asked, whence has it arisen that, in such a country as Ireland, the present calamity has been sufficient to disorganize the entire frame of society, and to set every sound principle of political economy at defiance ? Whence has it come to pass that, while England is illuminated by the glorious light of science, and the more glorious light of liberty—while England is blessed with knowledge, and strength, and power, and wealth, and happiness, Ireland is found still dark and desolate, not suffered to reflect the splendour, and profit by the bounty?   In answer to these questions, the writer of the following pages is excited by the crisis to state what appears to him to be truth.   He writes not for political party or religious sect—he writes for the country, to which he is bound by birth, by duty, and by affection.

DUBLIN, *6th January,* 1847.

THE

CASE OF IRELAND STATED.

———•———

THE state of Ireland, at a remote period, previous to the introduction of the English power, has been a subject of unmerited panegyric and unmerited abuse. The national vanity which emblazons doubtful pretensions in the splendid colouring of fancy, is not malignant in its origin, and is harmless in its effects; but the deliberate calumny which blackens the character of the injured, in order to justify or palliate the wrongs of the oppressor, deserves the severest reprehension of every friend to humanity and truth. However, Milesian antiquity and Milesian fame are, to the Irishman of the nineteenth century, a barren boast, a melancholy alleviation of injustice inflicted, and insult endured. Literary curiosity may be instructed or amused, and national vanity may be gratified by the real or fancied attainments of primitive independence; but in those events alone, by which his actual condition has been determined and must be affected, is man seriously concerned. The invasion of Ireland, by Henry the Second, is the first era in its annals which merits the deep recollection of the present times, and it is an era which must be remembered long. From

this period the series of events in Ireland may be traced
and connected as influencing essentially the character, the
fortune, and the hopes of the present generation, and it
may be of many generations yet to come.   These events
are important, not only as illustrative of the actual state of
things, but, perhaps, still more important, as pregnant
with speculation on the future.

When Ireland was invaded by Henry the Second, she
was in a state of internal disunion, disorder, and strife,
most favourable to the success of the invasion.   Had that
invasion not taken place, order might have succeeded to
confusion, liberty might have sprung from civil strife, and
strength from weakness.   Had Ireland—nearly girt by the
Atlantic, and embraced within the sphere of European
civilization and intelligence—been left as independent in
will as in station, is it to be conceived that she would, at
this day, exhibit the miserable contrast which she presents
to the opulence, the power, and the polity of England?
When England ceased to be a Roman province, though
invaded successfully by the Saxons, the Danes, and the
Normans, she still preserved national independence.   Superior in natural advantages to the countries of the invaders, she invited their rapacity or ambition, and fixed their
residence in her more eligible domain.   The Saxons and
the Danes were enterprising adventurers, seeking a settlement in a foreign land, not a provincial dependency to their
own.   William of Normandy was an adventurer of another
kind.   He aspired to the throne of an independent kingdom.   The battle of Hastings made him king of England.
By what is called the Norman Conquest, England only
changed a monarch; her national individuality remained.
But Ireland presented to the ambitious invader the sole
idea of a desirable accession to a feudal crown, and the

success of the invader necessarily involved the loss of national independence to the vanquished. The principle of
separate existence and individual growth was destroyed.
No sense of common interest, no talents and fortune of the
soldier, no wisdom and virtue of the sage, could be found
to unite the scattered elements of the people. There
is an interval of repulsion which precedes cohesion in political as in natural bodies. This interval is a moment of
weakness. The opportunity was observed and seized. The
native Irish—improvident, turbulent, and divided, brave in
battle, but rude in arms—continually sacrificing to personal
or family vengeance, every consideration of common safety
and general good, became the prey of invaders less rude,
and civilized enough to understand and employ the artifice
of profiting by disunion and converting the separation of
clans into national subjugation. *Divide et impera* is no
refinement in the policy of despotism. Unfortunately for
the cause of humanity, a sense of common good, and a wish
for common liberty, are too easily counteracted by exciting
or strengthening personal interest and jealous feeling. The
selfish and the malignant passions are so powerful in man,
that it requires no peculiar tact or skill, no master-strokes
of genius, no great dexterity of management, to make them
the instruments of his weakness and dishonour. The facility with which a number of Irish chieftains submitted to
the first English invaders is not surprising, but it was fatal.
An acquisition of territory, however small, and an acknowledgment of sovereignty, however partial, gained by Henry
the Second in Ireland, were, under the circumstances,
quite sufficient to secure to him, his heirs and successors,
the vassalage of Ireland for ages. It is idle to dispute
about the precise nature of the sovereignty with which the
English monarch was invested. It is idle to appeal to early

charters, or to triumph in early parliaments. The appeal
is delusive and the triumph vain. Charters and parliaments may be only the trappings of the slave. Evidence
stronger than that of charters and parliaments—evidence,
written in the tears and blood of the natives, exhibit Ireland, from the invasion of Henry the Second, as the pure
acquisition of conquest, begun, completed, and retained by
the sword. After the English had once secured a footing in
the country, the annihilation of Ireland, as an independent
state, was inevitable. The subjugation of the inhabitants
was difficult and tedious. Long after the doom of their
country had been fixed, the chieftains of some extensive
district, or numerous sept, stung with insult, provoked by
injury, roused by indignant feeling, tormented by the recollection of departed power, or impelled by the keen
sense of self-preservation, fought for vengeance or for
safety, and struggled for local independence, with a
frequency and an obstinacy which prolonged common
suffering, without the chance, or, indeed, the design of
effecting common emancipation. From inability, ignorance, prejudice, or private interest, no vigorous, comprehensive plan of conquest and civilization was ever adopted
by the invaders. Enough was done to secure provincial
subjection, but not enough to make that subjection either
profitable to the master, or comfortable to the slave.
Crude, desultory, unconnected schemes succeeded or
supplanted each other, according to the leisure, the resources, or the temper of the English Court, or the
character and talents of its deputies, without a knowledge
of the real value of the acquisition, or an enlightened and
liberal view either of colonial connexion, or provincial
dependence. The system of pale, and the vaunted system
of plantation, were founded on the cruel expulsion of the

natives from possessions dear to them from habit, and necessary for the support of life. War created national antipathies, and national antipathies terminated in the more deadly, and more lasting antipathies of religion. Owing to a variety of circumstances, after the Reformation, the Protestant religion became the religion of a large portion of the people of England, and was established as the religion of the state. In Ireland also, it was established by law as the religion of the state, while the Roman Catholic religion continued there to be the religion of the great body of the people. One cause alone seemed adequate to produce this effect. From the first, the Protestant religion appeared in Ireland, not recommended by reason and persuasion, but imposed by force—imposed by a power whose progress "in the beneficial work of conquering, and thereby breaking a savage nation to the salutary discipline of civil order and good laws," could be traced only by mangled corses and desolated plains. The right of private judgment in matters of religion is the sacred and irrefragable principle which justified the Protestant in renouncing the tenets and authority of the Church of Rome. But this right, the clear vindication of his own conduct, the Protestant respected not in others. The profession of Popery became highly penal. Hence arose a new and more permanent basis of English power in Ireland. By means of this division into two great religious sects—the Protestant comprising many subdivisions among its members—the English nation was more easily inflamed against the Irish people, and the Irish people more fatally armed against itself. The name of Papist became a sufficient apology for any act of injustice against the person who bore it, and the fury of bigotry was added to the desire of forfeiture in continuing a system of ruthless plunder and extirpation. It has been the curse of Ireland to derive no benefit from the wisdom or virtue of English sovereigns, yet to be the peculiar victim of their follies and their crimes. Elizabeth is the pride of English annals. But the conduct of Elizabeth, and her deputies in Ireland, was savage and impolitic in the extreme. The continued and merciless fury of her commanders drove the miserable natives to despair. Clemency was held to be incompatible with the fiscal interests of the crown. The acts of supremacy and conformity were imposed upon the people by force or fraud, and its attachment to Popery was increased and confirmed by persecution.

James the First was pedantic, conceited, hypocritical, and arbitrary. His favourite scheme of plantation could be carried into effect only by injustice. Severities were renewed in order to produce new insurrection and consequent forfeiture. But, notwithstanding frequent provocation and favourable opportunities, no considerable commotion took place in Ireland during his reign; yet the nobility and gentry of Ulster were stripped of their possessions without proof of treason; and in the other provinces the design was commenced, which was afterwards faithfully prosecuted, of seizing on estates under pretence of judicial inquiry into defective titles. The penal statutes were rigorously enforced by his express directions, and a barefaced course of oppression and extortion was practised, without control, in the ecclesiastical courts.

The character and conduct of Charles the First, marked by duplicity and arbitrary acts, were calculated to deceive the Roman Catholic, and to excite suspicion and distrust in the Protestant. His deputy, Wentworth, Earl of Strafford, haughty, despotic, and systematically faithless,

laid the foundation of the ills which followed.   Parsons,
and Borlase, connected with the parliamentarians, then the
prevailing party in England, aggravated the complaints of
the Roman Catholics, and, influenced by the most corrupt
motives, endeavoured to provoke a general insurrection.
The cause of the Roman Catholics, as a religious sect, contending for the free expression of those doctrines which
they professed, and the free exercise of that mode of
worship which they preferred, was founded on the rights
of conscience.   As Irishmen, provoked by wrongs, and
contending for the independence of their country, their
cause *might* have been founded on rights as sacred and
as clear.   But their views were sectarian, not national.
Their connexion with Charles the First, either as negotiat-
ing insurgents, or as allies, was wholly incompatible with
the idea of national emancipation; and their interests,
even as a party, were destroyed by their own dissensions,
and the interference of a vain, turbulent, and bigoted
foreign ecclesiastic. The attachment of the Roman Catholics to Charles the First arose chiefly from their dread of the
puritanical party in England and Scotland, which seemed
to threaten their religious tenets and worship with a
severer persecution than they had previously experienced.
That their views and conduct should be sectarian, and not
national, is not surprising, but their insurrection terminated,
as all former insurrections had done, in the extending and
confirming of the English power in Ireland.   In this
respect it was more ruinous in its effects than any that had
preceded it, by laying the deep foundation of that religious
animosity, and mutual intolerant bigotry, which well nigh
destroyed the natural sympathies and benevolent affections, by which men are held together in society.

Hypocrisy, genius, and courage raised Oliver Cromwell

to command—appointed chief of the parliamentarian forces in Ireland; his conduct there was marked by vigour and by cruelty. The strength of the Roman Catholics was entirely broken, and their discomfiture was followed by an inhuman proscription of their entire sect, in person and property. In the progress of events, the Roman Catholic cause had become identified with the royalist. The royalist cause embraced, at first, a number of Protestants as well as Catholics, but the two sects had never united with mutual confidence and affection. The Protestants were, without difficulty, detached from the king's party, and joined to the parliamentarians. Hence, the Roman Catholics (who composed the great mass of the Irish people) alone sustained the ruthless vengeance of Cromwell and his army. From the commencement of this insurrection to the restoration of Charles the Second, Ireland exhibited a scene of complicated woe. Whatever government prevailed in England, the great body of the Irish people were sure to suffer indignity and oppression, being constantly considered by the English nation as a conquered, dependent people, suspected, hated, and persecuted. Upon the restoration of Charles the Second, the Roman Catholics naturally expected an alteration in their favour. In this, however, they were disappointed. The administration of Irish affairs had always been considered in England a matter of temporary expediency only, never of justice. Whatever kind of policy seemed at the moment best calculated to secure the subjection and continue the weakness of Ireland, was adopted, without any regard to the rights, or any feeling for the sufferings of the natives; and upon this occasion it appeared politic to permit the mass of the people to remain, as they were found, plundered, oppressed, and degraded.

From the character of James the Second, Ireland was doomed to experience new calamities. His conduct in favour of the Roman Catholics there did not arise from the just policy of extending the benefits of legislation and government to all his subjects equally, without any distinction caused by difference of religious belief; it arose from a bigoted attachment to the Church of Rome, which he had displayed in an intemperate zeal for the re-establishment of Popery in England also, an attempt connected with his design of subverting the constitution and liberties of that country. His cause was espoused by the Roman Catholics of Ireland, not because he was a bigot, and wished to be despotic, but from a variety of motives, religious and political, independent of his mere personal character. Some of these motives influenced them in common with the Jacobites in England, who then composed no inconsiderable portion of that nation. Other motives arose from their particular situation, from a feeling of civil and religious degradation, and the natural desire of regaining the rank and property of which they deemed themselves unjustly deprived. But, whatever was its origin, the attachment of the Irish Roman Catholics to James the Second was unfortunate, in every view in which it can be considered. Success in the cause of such a man could not have effected any good national purpose for Ireland, and defeat more than ever fixed and confirmed the power of England in this country. The contest increased religious antipathies—victory inflamed the desire, supplied the means, and sanctified the continuance and extension of religious persecution; and the union of a people, whose only chance of independence rested on a combination of common feeling for a common purpose, seemed more impracticable and hopeless than at the time when Ireland was divided into a number of petty sovereignties and discordant septs.

The will of the people is the only rightful foundation of government. On this foundation the British constitution has been raised. The revolution of 1688, in England, derives its unanswerable vindication from this principle. To the practical application of this principle England is indebted for the liberty, the power, the wealth, and the glory which she enjoys. But the principle, its application, and its fruits, she has reserved to herself—her happiness has been incommunicable. The system of supporting English power, and administering English government in Ireland, has ever remained essentially unchanged.

The Revolution of 1688 gave or restored to England liberty and a constitution. The consequences of that revolution to Ireland were of a very different nature. To the Roman Catholic portion of the Irish people its consequences were disastrous. With respect to them, the Revolution of 1688 was followed by an increased penal code, unjust, oppressive, and impolitic in the extreme. In times of profound tranquillity, without the provocation of insurrection, or the pretence of conspiracy, laws of unexampled severity, affecting the Roman Catholic in mind, person, and property, attached to and entailed upon his religious belief, were rashly accumulated and rigidly enforced. Such a proscription of the great majority of a people is incompatible with the legitimate ends of civil association. Yet this proscription lasted long. It could not last for ever. A gradual relaxation in the penal code took place; entire emancipation was not effected till 1829. But, to relieve a sect from persecution is not giving liberty to a people. The Protestant and the Roman Catholic may possess equality of civil rights, and at the same time

share a common lot of political degradation. The civil
rights of person and property have been, and may be,
possessed, under domestic tyranny or foreign domination;
they may be possessed, but they cannot be *secured*—they
may be possessed, but they cannot be *enjoyed*.

Religious dissension has often disturbed the peace of
nations. It has been the bane of Ireland beyond every
other country in the world. In contemplating this afflic-
tion, all consideration of the respective merits of contending parties is lost in grief for their common infatuation.
Sad is the comparison which arises, not from the emulation
of virtue, but from the competition of folly or crime. That
such should be so long and so generally the state of man
in every clime, may well astonish the recluse, and pain the
philanthropist. Man, conscious of debasement, yet uncon-
scious of his rights and his strength—sensible of injury,
yet tamely submitting to wrong—spiritless and mean, in-
capable of understanding and asserting the high preroga-
tives of his nature—to be rational, to be moral, and to
be free—and making his own base and malignant passions
the instruments of his sufferings and his degradation.

The benefits resulting to England from civil strife, in
the triumph of liberty and the extension of trade, were
confined exclusively to herself. The shock of the conflict
had extended to Ireland, but was felt there only by the
havoc which it caused. Provincial dependence was the
basis of her political existence, and every event in her
history was assimilated to the life by which she grew.
The disunion of her inhabitants was the cause of her
original subjugation by England; and by the disunion of
her inhabitants, her dependence has been perpetuated and
secured. The disunion has continued; the causes of disunion have changed. The mutual jealousy of chiefs, the

blind vengeance of clans—hereditary feuds—distinction of colonist and native—English by blood and English by birth—had all their respective influence in the work of subjugation. But all these causes of evil were comparatively transitory and feeble; they had their day of desolation, and they ceased. The cause was forgotten, and the desolation might have been repaired. Religious bigotry succeeded, and remains. Potent and inveterate, blind and unforgiving, it embitters the present with the memory of the past—loads the living with the crimes of the dead—exalts creeds above practice—admits the evidence of mystery, rejects the evidence of fact, and prolongs hatred and hostility among those whom common suffering, common interest, and a common country, should unite firmly in sympathy, in affection, in object, and in action. The havoc of religious bigotry is worse than the havoc of war. The havoc of war is terrible, but temporary. It spreads destruction, but it does not annihilate the elements of reproduction; it violates the laws of humanity and the rights of nature, but it does not eradicate the principles upon which those laws and rights depend. It does not systematically corrupt the human heart; it rouses all its energies, and displays the heroism which saves, as well as the ambition which destroys. War has enthroned despots, but it has also given liberty to slaves. War is justified by self-defence against the wrongs of oppression. Religious bigotry is unmitigated evil.

————

From a view of the desolation of law the mind turns for relief to a history of the law itself. That history is important. The early grants and repeated confirmations of

English law to the Irish people, and the privilege of a distinct legislature in Ireland, have been appealed to as proofs that early national independence was established there by *compact*. The existence of such grants, and of such distinct legislature, may be clear and indisputable; but the inference is absurd. Had such compact been really made between the English invaders and the Irish nation, the observance of the compact by England would have furnished a literary curiosity—a singular anomaly in the history of ambition—a contract between the victor and the vanquished, securing freedom and independence to the vanquished, and religiously kept by the victor. The connexion between England and Ireland exhibits no such extravagant romance. Whatever compact did exist, or whatever benefits English law and a distinct legislature might confer, were long exclusively confined to the English colonists who had not *degenerated* by intermarrying with the natives, or by adopting their customs and manners, and to a few Irish septs who had been *enfranchised* by special favour. It is the honourable testimony of Sir John Davies, that "there was no nation under the sun that did love equal and indifferent justice better than the Irish, or would rest better satisfied with the execution thereof, although it were against themselves, so as they might have the protection and benefit of the law, when upon a just cause they did desire it." Sir Edward Coke, an English chief justice, loaded with law, but not over-burdened with liberality, also declares, "that there was no nation of the Christian world that were greater lovers of justice than the Irish, which virtue," he adds, "must necessarily be accompanied by many others." Yet, for the space of 350 years, at least, from the commencement of their subjugation, the benefit and protection of English

B

law were not communicated to the Irish, though they frequently desired to be admitted to that precarious privilege. The wish was counteracted by the English adventurers, in order that their cruelty and injustice to the natives might be indulged without restraint. The Irish were reputed aliens and enemies in their native land. It was adjudged no felony to kill them in time of peace. "The law did neither protect their life, nor avenge their death." When Henry the Second had once secured a firm footing in Ireland, whatever compacts he may have formed either with his own haughty and licentious barons, or with the native chieftains, can never be justly viewed in any other light than as the elements of a domination destined to comprehend both colonist and native in one common dependence. The most solemn engagements with the natives were sure to be violated, whenever the violation appeared necessary or useful to the extension of dominion; and, with respect to political privileges, the proud invaders soon became a feeble and dependent race. Charters and parliaments were to the Englishman in Ireland but precarious evidence of an unhallowed title to plunder and oppress. The insolent and rapacious foreigner was doomed eventually to feel, in common with the native, the humiliation which he caused; first the instrument, and finally the victim of conquest. Hence, in Ireland, internal distinctions among the people might be mutable in their nature, and controllable by events; but the external connexion with England was fixed and unchangeable—a necessary connexion of rule and dependency, of imperial authority and provincial subjection. On this relation between the superior and the dependent state, every change in the destiny of the dependent state immediately or remotely rested. Measures of legislation and measures of policy were either purposely devised for carrying out this principle of imperial authority and provincial subjection, or naturally took their tone and tendency from its powerful impulse. The conduct of England towards Ireland, considered as a dependent state, was unwise, illiberal, and unfeeling; but it was uniformly the conduct of the master to the slave. To represent the existence of early parliaments in Ireland, as a proof of early national independence, is a mockery of sufferings unexampled in severity, duration, and extent. The statute of Kilkenny—said to be so long quoted with reverence on account of its salutary provisions—is a memorable record of the nationality of those parliaments which, instead of wisely and humanely embracing the colonist and native within the protection of equal law, studied to mark more strongly the fatal line of distinction between them. The desire of the crown to impart, and of the native to receive, the protection of English law, was long withstood by those parliaments. Yet the people, whom they refused to incorporate into the body of subjects, whom in peace they would not govern by the law, and in war could not root out by the sword, such was their matchless injustice, they endeavoured to prevent from seeking refuge in a foreign country from the miseries of their own. By a statute passed in the reign of Henry the Fourth, it was ordained that no Irish *enemy* should be permitted to depart the realm without special license, and the person and goods of an Irishman attempting to transport himself without such license, might be seized by any subject, who was to receive one moiety of the goods; the other to be a forfeiture to the king.

The distinction between the English by blood and the English by birth, in Ireland, commenced in the reign of Edward the Third. The English by birth — the later adventurers—as they successively came over, affected to

despise and endeavoured to degrade the descendants of the
earlier invaders, or the English by blood. The English
by birth were favoured by the crown, as being more immediately devoted to its interests. But the English by
blood, from a long residence in the country, were more
numerous and more powerful than their adversaries. The
English by blood were attached to the house of York.
They even warmly espoused the cause of the impostor[*]
Simnel, and afterwards showed a disposition to favour the
pretensions of the impostor[†] Warbeck. But when Henry
the Seventh had borne down all opposition to his claims,
he took advantage of the dismay attending an abortive
attempt and disappointed wishes. The parliament in Ireland had been heretofore too much under the influence of
powerful deputies, and too much the instrument of turbulent factions, to be a ready and useful instrument of the
crown and English supremacy. Henry the Seventh, therefore, determined to new-model this parliament. This politic prince determined to reduce all factions in Ireland to
a state of common insignificance, and to simplify the exercise of foreign domination by making the Irish parliament
a mere court of record for recording the edicts of the sovereign power. This was effected by the celebrated law of
Poyning, which concealed its purpose under the fair appearance of correcting some acknowledged abuses, and did
not disclose at once its full and decisive effect on the future
power of the Irish parliament. Previous to this period,
the Irish parliament, such as it was, had claimed and
exercised the right of legislation, though interrupted by
occasional interference on the part of England, in the
same manner as the right of legislation was enjoyed by the
parliament of that country. The Irish parliament passed

* See Walpole's Historic Doubts.   † Idem.

laws for Ireland, with a negative power vested in the crown. But by the law of Poyning, made in the 10th year of Henry the Seventh, as afterwards explained and enlarged by the 3rd and 4th of Philip and Mary, the course of legislation was reversed. The original and efficient powers of legislation were essentially vested in the crown, and to the parliament was left a negative voice merely on the ordinances of the prince. Upon the construction of the statute of Poyning, and the explanatory act combined, neither the Lords nor Commons in Ireland had a right to frame or propose bills. The bill was first framed by the deputy and privy council of Ireland, was afterwards transmitted for approval to the king and council of England, who had a power of alteration, and of really making it a new bill, thenceforth unalterable, by sending it back under the great seal of England, and lastly it was presented to the Irish parliament, to which was left the single *privilege* of agreeing to the whole bill, as modelled and returned by the crown, or of rejecting it altogether, and thus remaining without any statute law whatever, except such as the parliament of England might think fit to impose. This practice was strictly observed until the reign of James the First, when the Irish parliament assumed a *privilege* of being humble remembrancers to the deputy and council in Ireland of what bills were proper to be transmitted to England. Hence arose the custom of framing, in either house of parliament in Ireland, what were called heads of a bill, which were carried up to the council there, from thence transmitted, if deemed fit by the council, and in the form of a bill laid before the king and council of England. Here it might be suppressed or altered at pleasure. If it was returned to the Irish parliament, the power of that parliament extended only to a simple acceptance or rejection of the bill, in the very form in which it came back, however changed from its original nature. Thus the high court of parliament in Ireland— the supreme *deliberative* assembly of the nation—was, in truth, little more than a public registry for the imperial rescripts of the English monarch and his privy council. The importance of Poyning's law as an instrument of provincial government, did not appear in full magnitude at once. The ministers of the crown in Ireland even contended on some occasions for a suspension of its provisions, as they happened to be influenced by a desire of extraordinary despatch, or some other temporary motive. And such was the miserable state of the Irish people, and such their dread of the power of a deputy, supported by a small parliament, composed of his own creatures, that every attempt on his part to dispense with this control over the parliament excited alarm, and a strict adherence to Poyning's law was long considered as the great security of the subject. But when—by the extension of the English conquest in Ireland—the business of parliament grew more weighty, and the number of the commons had increased, the ideas, both of the government and the people, changed. In the reign of Charles the First, the artful Strafford, who well understood the value of such an engine of power, admonishes his royal master that " the previous allowance of laws to be propounded in the Irish parliament, should be held as a *sacred* prerogative not to be departed from—in no point to be broken or infringed." A prerogative held sacred by a Strafford could have derived its sanctity only from a profanation of the rights of the people.

In England, the crown and the people, equally oppressed by the tyranny of feudal lords, conspired for its destruction, and succeeded. Restrictions on the alienation of property and feudal dependence were gradually abolished, commerce increased ; the commons rose, first, into wealth, and, finally, into power, which in its paroxysms subverted the monarchy, and in its more moderated energies established British liberty on the basis of the Revolution. But no change of circumstances could give useful life and vigour to the Irish parliament, as constituted by the law of Poyning. The commons might increase in number, wealth, and knowledge, but must still remain obscure and impotent. Such abject, mute submission to a foreign yoke debased their sentiments and paralyzed their powers. While that law remained, no permanent native vigour could ever mark the existence of that assembly. In England, with the Revolution of 1688, came liberty, and strength, and power, and science, and glory. The miserable province exhibited a sad and humiliating contrast of servitude and weakness—without a constitution, without trade—its people impoverished and divided— its parliament a motley compound of bigotry, pride, and meanness.

The law of Poyning may seem sufficiently to have marked the inferiority and secured the dependence of Ireland. It was an absolute surrender by her own parliament of its best powers. However injurious to the interest and degrading to the spirit of the people, it had become the rule of legislation in Ireland, and the acknowledged bond of her subjection ; but still it presented the idea of a distinct power, legislating for a distinct country, claimed as a right, and not held by mere sufferance. An explicit, open, undisguised declaration and exercise of sovereignty appeared necessary, fully to demonstrate the relation of imperial rule and provincial subjection. The policy of a Cæsar condescended to leave to an enslaved people the image of a free constitution. The policy was prudent; it was a sacrifice of pride to wisdom. But the individual despot will sometimes stoop to appearances, to which the despot nation will not bend. England disdained to govern Ireland by a dissembled authority. That England should govern Ireland by the parliament of Ireland was not enough. It remained to close the scene of conquest by a mortification of the feelings, as well as a triumph over the liberties of the conquered. This was achieved by an express declaration by the parliament of England, "That Ireland had been, was, and of right ought to be, subordinate to and dependent upon the imperial crown of Great Britain, and that the King and parliament of Great Britain had, and of right ought to have, full power and authority to make laws to bind the people of Ireland." Before this express declaration on the part of England, how did the matter really stand? The English parliament at a remote period had occasionally exercised the power of legislating for Ireland, particularly as to foreign trade, and some distinction had been taken, though it does not appear to have been practically attended to, between external and internal legislation. This occasional exercise of absolute legislative authority by England had generally been protested against by the Irish parliament as a usurpation. Indeed, the formal adoption by that parliament from time to time of laws previously enacted in England, and considered expedient in Ireland also, seemed to be a virtual admission that no law passed by the English parliament could, as such, have force in Ireland; and that, in order to give it validity there, the sanction of the Irish legislature was necessary; that the English parliament, though it might be followed as an example, was not obeyed as an authority. Thus much may be stated as matter of fact with respect to any exclusive legislative power claimed in ancient times by Irish parliaments.

But, in examining the political relation between England and Ireland, we must not be led away by formal grants of liberty, by pompous claims of right, by solemn protests against wrong. A country continually suffering, and bewailing and deprecating its sufferings in vain, furnishes a curious and extraordinary specimen of an independent power to be free and happy.

If it should be said that the invasion of Ireland by Henry the Second introduced into Ireland a distinct national legislature, mystically uniting it to the crown of England, and by that mystical union rendering it an independent kingdom, subject to the crown of England in the same way and to the same extent that England was subject thereto, and pursuing its own happiness according to its own will;—if this should be said, a man of plain understanding, acquainted with the relative condition of the two countries at the time of that invasion, with the opinion entertained by the invaders of themselves and of the people whom they invaded, and with the pious professions but real intentions of Henry the Second, might wonder exceedingly that such an admirable state of things should be the result of that invasion ; still, however, though disposed to be sceptical, he ought to yield to the weight of evidence and the force of truth. Let a view then be taken of Ireland from the close of the twelfth to the middle of the nineteenth century. If, throughout the whole of that period, the conduct of England to Ireland shall be found to exhibit Ireland as a constant scene of calamity and debasement—if, during the progress of a long protracted conquest, of inglorious victories and disastrous defeats,

Ireland shall appear covered with blood and desolation—
if, at the end of 150 years of undisputed subjection after
that conquest finally achieved, Ireland shall appear impotent, yet turbulent, *victa non pacata*, with a people ignorant and impoverished in an age of science, and a land of
fertile soil and genial climate—if such shall be the record
presented by indisputable facts, the faithful historian will
know how to appreciate the value of parchment fran-
chises—he will find England actually exercising the pre-
eminence of dominion, and Ireland enduring the wrongs
and the contumely of oppression, and he will conclude
that if Ireland cannot produce a better title than precedent to independence, she is of right enslaved.—But Ireland can produce that better title.—The title of man to
liberty rests on the nature of man—it rests on the
right of self-preservation, the first law of his nature. The
right of self-preservation in man is not the mere right of
preserving his animal life; it is also the right, the more
precious right by far, of preserving his moral and intellectual life, of preserving the free exercise of all those
powers and affections of soul which make his animal life
worth the having. Man is endowed with reason and conscience, is made a moral being, and gifted with an immor-
tal mind. By the glorious distinction of moral agency it
is that man is raised pre-eminent above the brute. The
moral nature of man is the source of his duties, is the
basis of his rights. The duties and the rights of man are
derived from heaven. To discharge those duties, and to
enjoy those rights, man must be free; and no man can
voluntarily become a slave without being guilty of a crime,
a crime against that Providence which has made him the
piece of workmanship he is, " noble in reason, infinite in
faculties—in action like an angel, in apprehension like a

god." No man, therefore, who has power to be free should submit to be a slave. The indefeasible record of independence is written by Deity on the mind of man. A charter of liberty is but evidence of an agreement to enjoy liberty according to certain forms. It never can be evidence of the right to enjoy. Even as evidence of the agreement, it derives its whole authority from the will of the people, which prescribes or consents to the mode. The charter of King John to the barons of England, at Runnemede, was but a record of the manner in which they wished to be governed by their kings. Their title to liberty rested not on the charter—it rested on THE RIGHTS OF MAN. Yet man seems to consider his title to liberty like his title to an estate, and anxiously inquires if his ancestors have registered the deeds. Man looks to antiquity for a right to be free; he might as well look to antiquity for a right to breathe. Man looks to antiquity for a right to be free, and is often a slave by precedent when he could not be made a slave by force.

But, be the precedents in favour of exclusive legislative power in Irish parliaments what they might, England respected them not. From time to time, as it served her policy, gratified her pride, or humoured her caprice, she legislated for Ireland. She regulated her trade, and disposed of her people and their property as she liked, regarding the Irish parliament as a subordinate assembly, subject to the interference and control of the superior state; and in proportion as Ireland increased in importance to England by the completion of conquest, and in proportion as England succeeded in her own struggles for liberty, her direct and open exercise of dominion over Ireland advanced to its full assertion and formal avowal. The instances of this direct exercise of dominion, from 1641 to

the Revolution of 1688, were frequent and flagrant. Whether England was ruled by a king, a parliament, or a pro-
tector—whether her government was a government of
prerogative, or of privilege, founded in right or in usurpation—her conduct to Ireland was the same; unvaried in
the despotic principles from which it flowed, varied only
by the difference of application which temporary expediency might suggest.

When, at last, by the Revolution of 1688, the political
dangers of England seemed to be at an end—when her
constitution seemed to repose securely after the tempests
by which it was shaken, had subsided—when, after a long and
doubtful struggle, the triumph of freedom in England
seemed to be complete, when success in that glorious cause
ought to have inspired the just and generous sentiment that
liberty was as dear to others as to herself—a change of
conduct with respect to Ireland might not unreasonably
have been suspected. It might have been expected, not
that England would abdicate her sovereignty, but that she
would exercise it with more feeling and less injustice.
That she would pay some regard to the wants, if not to
the rights of the province, and advance its industry while
she secured its dependence. It might have been expected that she would prefer the securing of that dependence through the indirect and less offensive means of an
Irish Parliament, rather than by the haughty assumption
of direct legislative supremacy, which insulted the slave,
without exalting the despot. If such expectations were
entertained by the sanguine or the credulous, disappointment quickly followed. The events which confirmed the
liberties of England seemed to stimulate her desire, as they
increased her power to oppress. The English Parliament
continued to legislate for Ireland. It legislated for Ire-

land, and ruined Ireland by legislation. It assailed her
manufactures and commerce, and, as it diminished the
value, so, with perfect consistency, it also diminished the
means of life.

––––––––

Not long after the Revolution of 1688 had seated
William the Third on the throne of England, Molyneux,
a member of the Irish House of Commons, roused by
some recent instance of legislation by the Parliament of
England highly injurious to his country, published his
celebrated "CASE OF IRELAND." This work deserves deep
attention. The author demonstrates that conquest could,
on no just principle whatever, give to England a rightful
dominion over Ireland. But England held Ireland by the
fact of conquest, and cared little about the *right*. Molyneux, it is true, denies even the fact of conquest, but
the denial is altogether unworthy of his talents and his
cause. He defines conquest to be, " an acquisition of a
kingdom by force of arms, to which force likewise has
been opposed." This definition is plainly erroneous. It
is not sufficiently comprehensive. Certainly, no peaceable
acquisition of a country by the free and voluntary submission of its inhabitants is, in the present argument, to be
defined a conquest. But the acquisition of a country by
the terror of force, without the actual infliction of force,
is just as much a conquest as an acquisition by force, to
which force has been opposed. It would not be easy to
distinguish between the acquisition of the robber who, with
a loaded pistol at your breast, makes you deliver up your
purse at once, and the acquisition of one who cannot compel
you to surrender the booty until after a struggle in which

you have been worsted. Indeed, Molyneux himself put this very case.—" If a villain," says he, " with a pistol at my breast, makes me convey my estate to him, no one will say that this gives him any right, and yet such a title as this has an unjust conqueror who, with a sword at my throat, forces me into submission." The man who gives up his estate or his purse from mere terror, may have less gallantry than the man who fights for them : and is beaten, but he is equally conquered and plundered.

Molyneux doubts not but the barbarous people of the island were struck with *fear* and *terror* of King Henry's *powerful force*, and yet, according to him, all was conducted with the greatest quiet, tranquillity, and *freedom* imaginable. He represents as *easy* and *voluntary* the submission of the natives, though struck with *fear* and *terror* of a *powerful force*, and concludes that there was no hostile conquest, " for where there is no opposition, such a conquest can take no place." But the error of Molyneux is not merely in his definition; his error is still greater in the application of his definition to historical facts. He admits that some of King Henry's vassals, by his *license* and *permission*, but not by his particular *command*, landed *hostilely* in Ireland, vanquished the natives in several engagements, and by that means secured an establishment in the country, upon which Henry, though he had not *commanded* the expedition, yet finding that his subjects had made *a very good hand of it*, came himself into Ireland, with an *army*, where he received from his successful subjects the fruits of their very good handiwork. Then comes the *free* and *voluntary* submission of the kings, princes, chiefs, archbishops, bishops, and abbots of all Ireland, swearing allegiance, and submitting themselves and their posterity for ever, to Henry, his heirs and successors, as true and faithful subjects; and here, according to Molyneux, terminates the acquisition of the entire kingdom with the greatest quiet tranquillity, and freedom imaginable. But what is the real case? Henry the Second, long before this magical acquisition of the dominion of Ireland, had meditated the conquest of it, and only waited for an opportunity and a pretence. When the pretence was afforded, being engaged in more urgent affairs himself, he permitted his subjects to embrace the opportunity which he had anxiously desired, and afterwards took advantage of their success obtained by actual force, to which force had unsuccessfully been opposed, and of the fear and terror caused by the presence of a powerful army, which he brought into Ireland with him. Had the matter terminated here, and had the acquisition been thus completed, it never could be considered as a peaceable acquisition by the voluntary submission of the natives. It would have been, to all intents, a hostile conquest. But the great perversion of facts consists in holding that the submission of the Irish chieftains, which Molyneux describes, is to be considered as a conversion of the entire body of the Irish people into liege subjects of the crown of England; that the scene of acquisition closed here, and that every subsequent conflict between the English invaders and the native Irish is to be viewed, not as a link in the chain of " acquisition of a kingdom by force of arms, to which force likewise was opposed;" but as a contest between a lawful prince and his rebellious subjects—subjects! whom the rapacious and sanguinary invaders for centuries denominated the Irish *enemy*—that the law might neither protect their life nor avenge their death—that they might be extirpated without restraint and without mercy; and so well was the wor of extirpation carried on, that, by the calculation of Molyneux himself, but a mere handful of the ancient Irish remained in his day—not one in a thousand; and Molyneux urges this very extirpation of the natives as an argument against the claim of any right by conquest over Ireland in his day, since thereby the great body of the people consisted of the progeny of English settlers, over whom, at least, England could have no lawful dominion by conquest, being the instruments of its attainments, not the objects of its inflictions. An attempt to prove that the subjection of Ireland to the English power has not been the effect of force, but the voluntary submission of its ancient people, is like an attempt to prove the non-existence of matter, the presence of which is evinced every moment of our lives by the testimony of every sense. No pompous or politic description of real or affected compact of submission—no misrepresentations of ignorant, weak, malignant, or prejudiced historians—no sophistry of argument advanced in the service of religious or political monopoly—no deliberate professions of the practical knave—no delusive misapprehensions of the honourable theorist, can ever repel or elude the irresistible conclusion from facts, that the dominion of England over this devoted land, is founded on a conquest as unprovoked in its origin, as hypocritical in its pretences, and, in its prosecution and completion as inhuman and inglorious, and in its consequences to the vanquished as calamitous, as ever stained the annals of ambition.

But, according to Molyneux, the victorious invaders and their posterity cannot be called a conquered people. They were not conquered by arms, but they were conquered by the force of moral causes. By the force of moral causes, the conquerors and the conquered were equally doomed to dependence. Their fortunes could not be separated. The victorious invaders were undone by their own victory. They conquered not for themselves— they conquered for England. They made Ireland a province, and the province made them slaves. That Ireland, subjugated as she was, could have retained national independence was a moral impossibility; that she did not retain it, is an historical truth, irresistibly pressed upon the mind by facts which cannot be controverted, and by a character which cannot be misunderstood.

Read that character in the champion of her rights; read it in a member of her insulted legislature; read it in a descendant of the victorious invaders; read it in Molyneux himself, the friend of Locke, whose genius he could admire, but whose spirit he could not imbibe, for Locke had a country and Molyneux had none—read that character in Molyneux himself;—

"If what I offer herein" (his 'Case of Ireland'), says he, "seems to carry any weight in relation to my own poor country, I shall be abundantly happy in the attempt; but if, after all, the great council of England resolve the contrary, I shall believe myself to be in an error, and with the lowest submission ask pardon for my assurance."

What! appeal from the demonstrations of reason to prejudiced, interested, proud authority, and model his belief by the rescripts of a parliament which was robbing his poor country of her trade, and her legislature of what he considered its ancient rights. What! ask pardon for daring to utter the conviction of his understanding and the dictates of his conscience in a cause which he felt to be the cause of truth and his country. Yes, Molyneux did live in a *conquered* country. While he denies the conquest by his argument, he proves it by his example. Molyneux did live in a *dependent* country; and while he appeals to fan-

c

cied liberty, we may appeal in himself to actual servitude. Indeed he admits, in express terms, the servitude which he endured, and seemed content to suffer :—

" Nor do I think," he says, " that it is anywise necessary for the good of England to assert this high jurisdiction (direct legislative supremacy) over Ireland. For since the statutes of this kingdom are made with such caution, and in such form as is prescribed by Poyning's statute 10 Hen. VII., and by the 3rd and 4th Philip and Mary, and while Ireland is in English hands, I do not see how it is possible for the Parliament of Ireland to do anything that can be in the least prejudicial to England."

Such is the reasoning of Molyneux; and beyond all controversy, under the statutes to which he refers, it was not possible for the Parliament of Ireland to do anything that could in the least be prejudicial to England. He might have added, with equal truth, that, under those statutes, it was not possible for the Parliament of Ireland to do anything that could be in the least beneficial to Ireland, without the permission of the superior state. The supreme will rested then, as it still rests, with England. What then, it may be asked, does this celebrated work of Molyneux shew. It proves incontestibly that conquest can give no *rightful* dominion to nation over nation. It proves the early existence of a *distinct* parliament in Ireland. That this parliament claimed, and generally exercised, an exclusive power of making laws for Ireland, considered its sanction necessary to give to acts of the English parliament a binding force in Ireland, and affected to treat any presumption to the contrary as an infringement of its privileges. Molyneux admits many late instances of interference by the English parliament in legislating for Ireland, but insists that they were unjust innovations. He

proves the existence of early grants and charters of liberty
to Ireland, and resists the claim of legislative supremacy
in the parliament of England to bind Ireland by its laws,
as contrary to precedent and principle. It rested with
the minister of England to decide the merits of the question. The minister of England clearly saw that it was not
a question of right, but a question of policy supported by
power. He well understood the nature of that distinct
parliament, for the privileges of which Molyneux strove.
He well appreciated the boasted grants of liberty which
Molyneux proclaimed. He well knew on whom they had
been conferred, and for what purposes they had been employed. He well knew how little England need regard
the instruments of conquest, after conquest had been
achieved. He well knew that the work of extermination
was but a work of substitution; that success had levelled
all distinctions but those which power might deem it expedient to create or maintain. But the British minister
did not wish to declare all those things. As England
possessed the supremacy of strength, he determined that
she should exercise the supremacy of legislation. But he
did not choose to publish her real title; he deemed it wise
to suffer that to remain concealed under the mysterious
confusion of ideas which different intellects, prejudices,
passions, and interests would be sure to throw around it.
He resolved that the right of legislative supremacy in
England should be assumed as something too evident to
be disputed, or too sacred to be discussed. The British
minister would, no doubt, have preferred precedent to mystery, and argument to assumption. But the precedents
were against him. In argument, "*The Case of Ireland*" was
unanswerable. It presumptuously assailed by reason what
policy required to be held an incontrovertible article of

faith. " *The Case of Ireland*" was committed by high authority, without trial, to the flames. Molyneux escaped!

———

When the nature of the Irish parliament, as modelled by Poyning's law, is considered—a parliament, impotent, abject, and composed of every element of dependence—an inquiry is naturally excited into the reasons why England should assume, and avow, and exercise the supremacy of direct legislation for Ireland.   It seemed unnecessary for maintaining a supremacy of will, by which she could always govern Ireland through the agency of an Irish parliament, and secure dependence without offending pride, or seeming to trench upon real or fancied privileges. It might be unwise, by recent usurpation, to provoke an examination into ancient *right*, which might itself be found to be, in fact, but an usurpation of an older date.   It might be dangerous to make dominion in its exercise too palpable to vulgar capacity, and too galling to be quietly borne by the tamest spirit.

For the slave without hope, it is enough to know that he is enslaved.   To investigate the causes of his ruin would be only aggravating his sufferings, without suggesting the means of relief.   But to the slave who may be free, and would be wise, a search into the motives of despotism,—which spring not from caprice, but design—not from accident, but system—not from temporary, but permanent causes,—ought to be interesting, and may be useful.

The greatness of England has arisen from liberty and from commerce.   The free government and free institutions of England may be considered more peculiarly her own.

The commerce of England may, at first, have sprung from, and in its growth and progress may have been intimately connected with, her free government and free institutions. But the commerce of England is a source of greatness depending more upon chance, and less upon will, more upon others, and less upon herself, than her constitution, government, and laws. Commerce is a good, not absolute, but comparative and dependent. The relations of commerce are infinite. It is connected with, and dependent upon, not only the geographical position and internal physical properties of different countries, but it is also connected with, and dependent upon, the knowledge and the ignorance, the opinions and the prejudices, religious and moral, political and financial, of different countries. It depends much upon design, and much upon accident—much upon wisdom, and much also upon fortune. In contemplating the position of England, as well absolute as compared with other states, we are led to consider her chiefly in a commercial point of view. In estimating her character as a nation, we no doubt observe the constitution of her government, and the spirit and administration of her laws, as distinguishing her in an eminent degree above other nations. But it is in the influence which the constitution of her government and spirit of her laws may have had upon her general policy in peace and war, as connected with foreign powers, or her own dependencies, that those powers and dependencies are chiefly concerned. As an object of speculative inquiry, or practical imitation, the British constitution may be calculated to delight and to improve mankind, while British policy may have derived from that constitution but the motives and the means of injustice and oppression. It is not by her existing power merely that we are to measure the greatness of England,

but by that power compared with her native strength.
England does not possess in herself independent greatness
from extent of territory and fertility of soil, and consequent population.   Her colossal power rests mainly on
external commerce ; and other nations are chiefly interested in her constitution and laws, as that constitution
and those laws have been connected with her commerce,
and as her foreign policy has been connected with all.
" Perish commerce—live the constitution !" when applied
to England, have been justly considered foolish words:
And if the constitution and commerce of England have
grown and must fall together, and if her policy rests the
security of both upon unjust aggression and foreign domination, respect for her constitution will excite no sympathy in the diminution or subversion of her commercial
greatness.

But our inquiry into the policy of England must be limited to a view of the nature and motives of her conduct
to Ireland in the haughty assumption of a right to bind
Ireland *directly* by her own laws, and an intemperate depression of the Irish people.   The connexion between
England and Ireland—always a connexion of rule and dependency—had been modelled originally by the circumstances of the times.   It commenced in feudal times, and
in its progress it exhibited the uncertainty which marked
those times.   The manner in which the conquest of Ireland
was effected, by the intervention of English settlers, who
claimed the privilege of carrying with them the rights of
Englishmen, necessarily produced charters and parliaments
and the forms of constitutional liberty in a country which
experienced, in fact, the most humiliating servitude.   The
power of England, for a long time, comparatively strong,
but really feeble, rendered a vigorous plan of conquest im-

possible. A conquest, prolonged from this weakness in England, through many years of calamity and disgrace, was subject to the vicissitudes of capricious, temporary, unconnected schemes. The original design of conquest, which might have been defeated by union among the natives, was unskilfully, but obstinately persevered in, and finally completed. It had been conceived in an age of rude, desultory warfare, in the mere spirit of acquisition, with a determination to subjugate the invaded country, but without any precise fixed object in the subjugation. Hence the idea of dependency was constantly connected with Ireland in the English mind. This must ever be the case between the victors and the conquered, when they continue after as before the conquest—distinct people in distinct countries. But though the idea of dependency was invariably associated with Ireland in the English mind, and this association led to an unqualified exercise of dominion on the part of England over Ireland, no clear and accurate idea appears to have been formed for a length of time by English princes or English statesmen of the manner in which this same dependency of Ireland could be best fashioned and administered for the benefit of the ruling state.

Before any precise notions of political liberty had been formed in England, the feudal barons, who came from thence to settle in Ireland, carried with them such notions upon this subject as then prevailed, and the *formal* basis of such a constitution as England then possessed. But after some time it was discovered that in this *formal* basis of a constitution, too much had been conceded to Englishmen in Ireland. When the English settlers had been so long and so firmly established in the country as apparently to secure the acquisition; when retreat seemed to be destruction to them, and their safety and continuance there

absolutely dependent on England, it was then discovered
that a parliament in Ireland, similar, even in form and
figure, to that of England, was too formidable in faction to
be useful to despotism. Poyning's law repaired this defect.
By this law was introduced a settled form of subjection,
and an established organ by which imperial will might
communicate its mandates. But in the occasional paroxysms of domination, or in the confusion of troubled times,
even this form of provincial government was violated. And
at length the violation of principle, when that violation
appeared conducive to the aggrandizement of England,
came to be considered by the English parliament as itself
a principle, or as grounded upon antecedent principle,
which it would be presumptuous to controvert or even to
doubt.

But whence arose this change in the policy of England ?
Whence did it arise that England, not satisfied with the
instrumentality of the Irish parliament in ruling Ireland,
assumed a power of direct, immediate, imperial legislation
over it? This change arose from that revolution in the
circumstances of Europe which substituted trade for chi-
valry, and commercial enterprise for feudal violence, but
unaccompanied by a knowledge of the true principles upon
which trade and commerce depend. When England, peculiarly fitted for commercial pursuits, and formed for commercial greatness, had directed her views to the attainment
of this, her natural state, it seemed, according to the narrow trade-policy of the times, that a legislative body in
Ireland, possessing even a negative voice on imperial regu-
lations of the trade of Ireland, might be an obstacle to the
unrestrained exercise of dominion which the interests of
commerce might require. Were Ireland left to the free
exercise of her native strength, no reasonable doubt could

exist of her success. The Irish parliament, it is true,
during the continuance of Poyning's law, unless permitted
by the English cabinet, could not encourage Irish trade,
and promote Irish manufacture by active protection; but
in general, perhaps, commerce flourishes most where least
encumbered by legislative interference. Ireland certainly
did labour under severe adventitious depression, and required the fostering care of a wise and patriotic legislature
to assist in raising her to her just position in the scale of
national existence. Still, however, such is the vital power
of Ireland, that she must have advanced rapidly in growth
and vigour, if her parliament, impotent to create, should
not be active to destroy; but, by mere neutrality, leave her
to the bounty of heaven, to industry, and to fortune. But,
from Poyning's parliament neutrality could not be expected; and England, through that parliament, carried on
active and deadly hostility against the manufactures and
trade of Ireland, directly by commercial prohibition; indirectly by religious persecution. But even that parliament,
though shackled and debased, formed some barrier against
the unfeeling policy of another state, which viewed Ireland
at once in the double light of a dependent and a rival. Even
that parliament, from a sense of self-importance, from an
identity of interest with the body of the people, would have
been in some degree restrained from entering blindly into
the views, and gratifying, without limit, the fears, the prejudices, the ignorance, and the avarice of the British manufacturer and merchant, and sacrificing to the ephemeral
popularity of a British minister all the present good and
future hopes of Ireland. An attachment to country will
cling to and actuate the basest minds, unless overcome by
powerful personal interest; hence would exist the trouble-
some and expensive necessity of constantly maintaining

this powerful counteraction. . Or, perhaps, an attachment, to country is, in sordid minds, but an attachment to self, to some personal advantage enjoyed from the country, unconnected with social feeling and public good. Such vileness must be bought, and self made to outweigh self. The parliament of Ireland, through which English rule in Ireland was to be maintained, appeared to be somewhat impracticable, with respect to Irish trade. The prejudices of this parliament were favourable to the British policy of sectarian division; but its interests were against the British policy of national impoverishment and depression. This parliament could be induced, without difficulty, to enact severe penal laws against the Irish Roman Catholics, but was reluctant to destroy the Irish woollen manufacture. This would not satisfy the policy of England, by which a double object was to be secured—keeping Ireland weak by the poverty of the people, and still weaker by their division. The first object could be most easily attained through the English parliament; the latter through a domestic legislature. The prejudices of the English parliament would be all in favour of British monopoly in trade, the prejudices of the Irish parliament in favour of the British policy of exciting the Protestant against the Roman Catholic, and thus debilitating both. Indeed, by this blind, intolerant spirit in the Irish parliament, that parliament was the instrument, also of the commercial jealousy of England. If the religion of the Roman Catholic was really, with the Irish parliament, the only object of penal enactment against it, the industry of the Roman Catholic, though indirectly, was thereby much more fatally assailed. A rare and solitary convert might now and then proclaim the triumph of terror or corruption, while an ignorant, a bigoted, and a starving population exhibited the necessary, the constant, and the permanent effects of an unjust and impolitic code.

Thus, by the assumption of legislative supremacy in the parliament of England, binding Ireland by its laws, whatever benefits to Ireland the Irish parliament might wish to spare or secure could be at once diminished or destroyed, and Irish talent and Irish industry crushed or directed, as should appear best calculated to promote the commercial views of England, however erroneous in commercial principle those views might be; while the parliament of Ireland would answer the subordinate purposes of provincial legislation, limited not only in its virtual, but in its formal powers; and exhibiting the appearance as well as enduring the reality of subjection, acting by a delegated authority, and, by the very abuses of that authority, securing the permanence of the dominion under which it served. This right of supreme legislation in England as the superior state, being once assumed, necessarily implied the right of exercising the power in any case, according to the impulse of ambition, the temptations of interest, the suggestions of prudence, or the whims of caprice; and the Irish parliament could be considered as existing by sufferance only, and permitted to continue in existence from policy alone. That parliament was destined, in one short hour of convulsive strength, in one short hour of passing glory, to humble the pride and alarm the fears of England. It was also doomed to perish for ever by the policy which it thus once dared to disappoint and provoke. But, before that bright hour of its triumph, and that fatal period of its doom arrived, England continued to employ the Irish parliament in the drudgery of domestic routine legislation, or in the more vigorous, but more disgraceful, office of civil and religious persecution.

But why should England thus labour to depress and impoverish Ireland so much more than seemed to be necessary for her own safety, and so much more than seemed to be consistent with her own interest? Would not wisdom prescribe a more enlarged and generous policy? Must not the extreme weakness and poverty of Ireland defeat the rapacity which demanded the sacrifice, and enfeeble the power which triumphed in the desolation? When England had subdued the country and formed the province, why could she not, like ancient Rome, govern with authority, but govern without fear—destroy independence, but not destroy the means by which the slave may be well housed, well clothed, and well fed? That England might by a wise and liberal policy have given to Ireland happiness and to herself strength, and exhibited the rare union of conquest and moderation, of power and justice, was within the limits of moral contingency. That England would have oppressed with a milder tyranny, might have been expected from the cold calculations of political prudence. But a comparison of the natural powers and capacities of the two countries, which strikingly indicated a competition of strength—the consciousness in England of accumulated wrongs—the dread of long-protracted vengeance—the pride of power—the jealousy of commerce, when its true principles were little understood—all conspired to produce on the part of England a policy, narrow, suspicious, selfish, and sanguinary. Ireland had been conquered without any settled statesmanlike plan of conquest on the part of the victors, and, throughout the entire duration of her subjection, she has exhibited not only an opposition between form and reality, but the more extraordinary opposition of servitude and rivalship. By nature a rival, by fortune an appendage to England, the bounty of nature has been her curse—the equal has been punished in the slave. A conviction of what Ireland might do, and ought to do, seems to have impressed upon the policy by which her destiny has been controlled a character of fear and severity, pride and meanness, jealousy and suspicion, unexampled in the annals of provincial administration.

The history of ancient Rome, from her humble origin to the zenith of her power, presents, with few exceptions, a scene of extensive and splendid conquest. The imagination is dazzled with the renown of high military achievement, and the mind is elevated by the contemplation of ardent devotedness to country. But we are not merely astonished with the number and magnitude of her victories, and charmed with the patriotism of her citizens—we are also instructed by the wisdom of her institutions, which gave proportion, and harmony, and strength, and permanence to the solid fabric of her greatness—and we ascribe the conquests of Rome not to fortune, but to genius. The Romans were trained to conquest upon a system uniform and comprehensive. The design of universal dominion could only have been gradually inspired by successive triumphs, but the policy which led to and long maintained that dominion was early formed and steadily pursued, and seemed to gain strength from occasional defeat. It was simple and grand, capable of universal application—not depending on individual talent, rarely occurring or capriciously applied, nor on the varying impulse of the people. Domestic struggles terminated in a well-constructed government, and domestic peace gave greater energy to foreign exertions, but the institutions more immediately connected with conquest continued their uniform operation, undisturbed by political storms.

The imperious policy of war controlled all parties and combined all talents. The unity of conquest was preserved entire. In maintaining the honour, enlarging the boundaries, and advancing the glory of the Roman empire, the efforts of the Roman people were common, voluntary, ardent, and persevering. As other countries were successively subdued by the Roman power, they were deprived of distinct national existence and national freedom; but, once deprived of independence, they were no longer considered distinct objects of apprehension or jealousy. By a singular and happy policy, universally applied to all parts of the empire, the fortune of the provinces was identified with the fortune of the ruling state; and Rome, with her original territory, and her acquisitions by war, seemed to be all blended together into one mighty mass of consolidated strength and greatness.

The provinces were, no doubt, enslaved; but Rome, with a wise and intrepid policy, permitted them to enjoy every advantage not absolutely incompatible with her views of universal empire, and freely imparted to them the benefits of her superior advancement in knowledge, laws, and manners, or freely borrowed from them the sciences, arts, or literature in which they respectively excelled. The provinces were degraded by subjection, and must have felt the degradation—they were oppressed, and must have felt the oppression; but that degradation and oppression were only such as seem to be inseparable from the loss of national independence—they were the necessary incidents of subjection, not the studied aggravations superinduced by jealousy and fear. The Roman province was not debased and impoverished upon system; the principle according to which it was governed was not a principle of deterioration. Independence was destroyed, but the fountains of social happiness were not poisoned; industry was repressed by taxation, but not prohibited by law. Each province was held in obedience by the united force of the empire, and ruled by one common law of domination, applied without distinction and without distrust. The idea of jealousy, arising from rivalship or competition of interests, between the superior state and the provinces, could not exist. The despotism of Rome over her dependencies, was not the despotism of envy or suspicion; it was the despotism of a power which, having formed the design of universal conquest, was taught by success to consider itself irresistible, and which viewed every new acquisition as an accession of strength, not an object of apprehension. The vanquished countries, with their inhabitants, their wealth, their resources, and their capabilities, were embraced within the common circle of empire, interest, and protection. In the loss of independence they lost the ennobling consciousness of freedom of will; but the loss was not aggravated and embittered by the petty, vexatious, malignant hostility of a suspicious tyranny.

The subjects of a government absolute, but wise and fearless, consistent and temperate, the provincials were ruled, not persecuted; deprived of liberty, they were not also deprived of ease, they were permitted to enjoy, without envy and without restraint, all the happiness which could be enjoyed by men who had fought for and lost—but not ignobly lost—national independence. Rome and her provinces formed one consolidated body, and when barbarian hordes successively poured in upon, and finally broke to pieces the mighty mass, the provinces lay prostrate—the scattered fragments of departed greatness. Had the reduction of Ireland to the state of a Roman pro-

vince completed the extensive plan of Agricola, we might
have been able to demonstrate, by the contrast of facts
applied to Ireland herself, the difference between the
condition of a dependency of Rome, and a dependency of
England. By the melancholy comparison of the servi-
tudes of Ireland herself, we might have been able to demonstrate the superior misery of being subject to a power
sufficiently strong to conquer and oppress, but not sufficiently noble to be above jealousy and suspicion. It is a
dangerous policy which, by the very means employed to
enfeeble and debase, instructs its victim in the secret of
his strength, and the remedy for his misfortunes. It is a
dangerous policy which betrays the fears, while it inflicts
the wrongs of oppression. By exposing the weakness as
well as the injustice of despotism, the exercise of severity
seems necessary to the preservation of the despot. When,
in the history of his ruin, the slave has been taught a
lesson of deliverance, the tyrant can see no safety but
in increasing the weight of chains, the slave no relief from
suffering but in death or emancipation.

Lord Littleton, in his history of Henry the Second,
after mentioning an unsuccessful attempt of the conquest
of Ireland, by Magnus, King of Norway, in the beginning of the twelfth century, makes the observation following—"If this enterprize had been wisely conducted, and the
success had been answerable to what the divisions among
the Irish princes and the inclination of the Ostmen in
favour of a monarch, from whose country most of them
originally came, seemed reasonably to promise, it would
have erected, in Ireland, a Norwegian kingdom, which, together with Man and other dominions of Magnus full of
shipping and good seamen, might, in process of time, have
composed a maritime power capable of maintaining itself,

perhaps for ever, against that of the English, and disputing with them the sovereignty of the sea.   It may, indeed, be esteemed most happy for this nation (England) that no King of Denmark, or of Norway, or of Sweden, nor any prince of the Ostmen settled in Ireland, ever gained an entire dominion of that isle, for had it remained under the orderly government of any of these, its neighbourhood would have been, in many respects, prejudicial to England."   This work of Lord Littleton is said to have engaged his attention, and to have been under his revision for twenty years before its publication, and such is the conclusion which, after mature reflection, he draws from the relative situation of England and Ireland.   Indeed, the formidable aspect of Ireland, presented to view as an independent state, appears to have made a strong and fatal impression on the counsels of England, at an early period.   In the reign of Elizabeth, the infamous policy of ruling Ireland by means of her intestine divisions, her barbarism, and her poverty, was openly avowed by the ministers of that unfeeling princess.—" Should we exert ourselves," said they, " in reducing this country (Ireland) to order and civility, it must soon acquire power, consequence, and riches.   The inhabitants will be thus alienated from England, they will cast themselves into the arms of some foreign power, or, perhaps, erect themselves into an independent and separate state.   Let us rather connive at their disorders, for a weak and a disordered people can never attempt to detach themselves from the crown of England."   It is true, that Sir Henry Sydney and Sir John Perrot, who perfectly understood the affairs of Ireland, and the disposition of its inhabitants, a generous disposition easily won and attached by kindness, expressed the utmost indignation at such abominable maxims,

D

" Yet this doctrine found it way," says the historian, " into the English Parliament."

Certainly it did, and that was not the first era of its appearance in that parliament. From the time that Ireland can be said to have seriously engaged the attention of the English government, the doctrine of keeping Irishmen quiet, not by voluntary attachment, but by hopeless debility, uniformly pervaded its councils, while the English Parliament, untouched by individual pity, unrestrained by the sense of individual honour, or the feeling of individual shame, as is too often the case with bodies of men, was found ready to execute and even to anticipate the worst purposes of this inhuman policy of depression. This jealousy towards Ireland increased with the increasing commerce of England. It was impressed upon the measures of each successive Minister, not merely by his own prejudices and fears, but by the more intemperate prejudices and fears of the English people. A minister of genius, intrepidity, and virtue might soar above the narrow and barbarous policy of ages. But the fate of Ireland rested not even on the remote and precarious chance of a generous and wise administration. It rested on the passions, the prejudices, the ignorance, the pride, the obstinacy, the avarice, and love of power of an entire people. The boasted pre-eminence of the British constitution, in giving effect to the popular will in the administration of public affairs, to the English nation a cause of triumph, was to the province a source of calamity and humiliation. In the progress of the commercial aggrandizement of England an intimate connexion was formed between the state and the trading interest of the nation. The trading interest gained a complete ascendancy over every other interest. It not only received a peculiar, constant, and anxious protection, but the most unreasonable desires and apprehensions of the English merchant, manufacturer, and mechanic were attended to, and flattered by the English minister, and the English parliament. The power of the English merchant, manufacturer, and mechanic, multiplied the wrongs, perpetuated the dependence, and aggravated the mortifications of Ireland. In acts of foreign tyranny the English minister was the faithful servant both of the crown and the people, and in acts of foreign tyranny, the English House of Commons faithfully represented its constituents. To increase the commerce of England seemed to be a sufficient motive and justification for any act of injustice or aggression towards other nations, and its own dependencies. Had Ireland been less the favourite of nature, she would have been less the victim of policy; but her natural advantages, her geographical position—her temperate climate—her fruitful soil—her hardy peasantry—her rivers, lakes, and harbours—numerous and commodious—and all the other proofs of her independent structure and vital power, which impressed the ministers of Elizabeth with the well-founded opinion, that possessed of a good government, she must soon acquire intelligence, wealth, and happiness, seem to have fixed her fate and marked her for destruction.

The maxims of these ministers, though not directly avowed, were embraced and followed by their successors, and the effects may be easily traced in characters deep and lasting. Had Ireland been less formidable by nature, England might have been less unjust both to Ireland and to herself. The contracted policy, and dastardly spirit of rule, filled with the constant dread of competition in trade, not only made the province desolate, but marred the fortunes of the empire.

Instead of the wise, and grand, and magnanimous principle of comprehending Ireland within the sphere of England's hopes and fears, interests and aspirations, aggrandizement and glory, the narrow, selfish, mean, and dangerous principle of exclusion was adopted.

IRELAND MUST NOT BE INDEPENDENT, was a resolution which involved an odious train of base motives, and malevolent acts. It was a resolution which excited and kept up in the mind of those who had the power of dispensing good or inflicting ill, a constant feeling of jealousy and apprehension. It seemed to put a negative on the communication of happiness—to limit the art of government to petty, temporary expedients of prevention, and fitful, cruel, remedies of force, and to confine the objects and benefits of conquest to the mere extinction of a rival. And it may be asked, is not that advantage great? Would not the absolute physical extinction of Ireland, by some violent convulsion of nature, be to England a subject of gratulation compared to the existence of Ireland as a free and independent country? Such, indeed, does appear to have been a question ever present to the mind of British statesmen, and to keep Ireland impotent and dependent has been the bound of their ambition in this department of their cares. That nature, in assimilating the powers, had contrasted the interests of England and Ireland, seems to have been an article of belief, which precluded any attempt by English sovereigns or English ministers to unite the countries by sympathy of affection, derived from a participation in common rights, common enjoyments, and common protection. The haughty pride of conquest could not stoop to equality of rights; the contracted spirit of commerce could not conceive, or would not tolerate a community of interests.

The principle of KEEPING IRELAND DOWN was the only

principle which could satisfy the pride and quiet the prejudice of Englishmen—which could reconcile all contra-
dictions, allay all fears, please all fancies, indulge all passions, and silence all complaints. But in this conspiracy
of weak, sordid, and malignant motives against her peace,
Ireland might learn to value and respect herself—to know
that strength which could excite the apprehensions, alarm
the jealousy, and provoke the persecution of her oppres-
sors. Ireland, in her humiliation, might learn a lesson of
ambition. The nation which is feared ought to be aspiring.

From the Revolution of 1688, a memorable era in the
history of the British constitution, the parliament of Ireland exhibited a spectacle of abject debasement. Humbled
to the condition of a subordinate legislature, even the limits
of its circumscribed authority were not ascertained by any
fixed distribution of powers and privileges, but depended
on the undefined and arbitrary will of the superior state.
Whenever the English parliament deemed it expedient to
interfere, either in its legislative or judicial capacity, its
will constituted at once the principle and the justification.
The feeble and transient complaints of the Irish parliament were treated with contempt. Yet this parliament,
thus insulted and degraded, became the miserable instrument of the tyranny which oppressed it. More disho-
noured by its own passions than by the despotism to which
it bowed, the period of its greatest servitude was the period
of its greatest injustice. At the very period when the
Irish parliament complained of the infringement of its own
privileges, and the destruction of Irish commerce, it out-

raged the rights of nature, and assailed the duties of social life. In a country beggared and debilitated by the laws of a foreign power against its trade, its domestic legislature enacted laws ruinous to the peace, the morals, and the industry of its people.

This domestic legislature, impotent to protect, but powerful to persecute, and uncontrolled in persecution, was at last by the English parliament declared *expressly* to be what it had long *virtually* been, the mere dependent instrument of foreign domination.

By an English act of parliament, 6 Geo. I. c. 5, passed in the year 1719, entitled " An Act for the better securing the Dependency of the kingdom of Ireland upon the Crown of Great Britain," it was declared, " That the kingdom of Ireland hath been, is, and of right ought to be, subordinate unto, and dependent upon, the Imperial Crown of Great Britain, as being inseparably united and annexed thereunto; and that the king's majesty, by and with the advice and consent of the lords spiritual and temporal, and Commons of Great Britain, in parliament assembled, had, hath, and of right ought to have, full power and authority to make laws and statutes, of sufficient force and validity to bind the kingdom and people of Ireland. And that the House of Lords of Ireland had not, nor of right ought to have, any jurisdiction to judge of, affirm, or reverse any judgment, sentence, or decree, given or made in any court within the same kingdom, and that all proceedings before the said House of Lords upon any such judgment, sentence, or decree, were thereby declared to be utterly null and void to all intents and purposes whatsoever." The true intent and meaning, force, and effect of that memorable statute, no dulness could misunderstand, no sophistry could explain away. By that statute, the parliament of

England, with imperious solemnity, ratified all its past usurpations, and recorded the high prerogative of strength to tyrannize over weakness. Whatever ideas of self-importance the provincial legislature might, theretofore, have indulged, were by that statute completely dispelled. The dream was ended, the phantom vanished, and the parliament of Ireland awoke to a perfect sense of its insignificance. From thenceforth that parliament could not mistake the nature and extent of its tenure. The same power which had proclaimed its dependence might destroy its existence. When it was declared, " That the British parliament had, and of right ought to have, full power and authority to make laws and statutes of sufficient force and validity to bind the kingdom and people of Ireland," it was, in fact, declared, that the Irish parliament existed only by sufferance, as the delegated instrument of those menial offices which the British parliament might consider beneath its dignity, or unworthy of its regard, or of those works of desolation which the British minister might think best suited to the prejudices and passions of the provincial assembly.

By the statute, 6 Geo. I. c. 5, the authority of the British parliament to bind Ireland by its laws, was assumed to be an authority, original, universal, absolute, and without control. And while this statute remained the recorded declaration of British sway, it is plain beyond controversy, that the parliament of Ireland was permitted to legislate in any case from policy merely. As the parliament of England was declared to have a *right* to legislate in every instance, the parliament of Ireland could have but a *license* to legislate in any instance, and could be permitted to exercise that license, only the better to promote the objects of the power which arrogated the right. It is rather a curious circumstance, not unworthy of remark, that previous to the passing of the 6 Geo. III. c. 5, the Union between England and Scotland had been effected, by which representatives of Scotland were to sit both in the English House of Lords, and the English House of Commons, and from thenceforth were to have a voice in making laws: It is not pretended that Scotland conquered, or assisted England in the conquest of Ireland, and yet by the 6. Geo. I. c. 5, Scotland was to share in the power of making laws for Ireland.

Upon the same principle, if, previous to the 6 Geo. I. c. 5, England had admitted the Island of Jamaica to send representatives to the English parliament, the master of the negro slave, the owner of the bloody lash, by which that slave was tortured, would, as such legalized and constitutional butcher, have a clear and indefeasible right to make laws for the government and discipline of the serfs of Ireland.

While the friend of freedom disdains to advocate the cause of the Irish parliament, which submitted to such ignominious bondage, he must sympathize in the fate of the Irish people, doomed, through all the changes of British policy, to endure the curse of servitude, and the contumely of oppression, and he will seize every opportunity which the history of that policy presents to investigate its motives, reprobate its injustice, and expose its weakness.

The great object of England was commercial ascendancy; most of her dependencies, from situation and productions, seemed to be naturally excluded from competition, but calculated to consume the produce of British industry, and to return what British wants or British luxury might demand, or British enterprize might diffuse, either in its original state, or with the additional value imparted by ingenuity and art, and which the wants or luxury of other countries might finally use or waste. But Ireland, in every point of view—in vicinity, insular advantages, soil, climate, productions, and people, presented the constant haunting idea of competition. Ireland forced upon the mind the striking picture of a country, the inhabitants of which would easily fall into and form the three great classes of agriculturists, manufacturers, and merchants, from whose united exertions and pursuits, both internally and in relation to other states, must necessarily have flowed wealth, power, and independence, if Ireland were left to the free, unconstrained use and application of her own resources, physical and intellectual. Happy in the facility of supporting a number of laborious hands, in the means of a varied and abundant agriculture, in many productions of nature, the raw materials of art, in a hardy and ingenious people, capable of adding to these materials, or to the productions of other climates, the incalculable value of industry and skill, Ireland, like England, seemed formed by nature to supply the wants, or minister to the comforts of other states. Placed on the western skirt of Europe, with three-fourths of her shores washed by the Atlantic, after the discovery of a new world had opened to European enterprize new objects of adventure, and new sources of aggrandizement, Ireland seemed destined to be an important connecting link in the intercourse between the Eastern and Western hemispheres. Independent of the discovery of America, and the new field thereby opened for commercial enterprize, the situation of Ireland seemed peculiarly fitted for maritime pre-eminence, not only cast, as she is, between England and the West, but also possessing greater facilities of communication with the East, and many parts of Europe. Ireland, too, had before her many glorious examples of what free states, very inferior to her in extent of territory, and other natural advantages, could achieve by commercial daring. The powers of independent existence seemed to be marked in her structure in such bold characters, by nature, that it required the unceasing efforts of an active and malignant policy to defeat the obvious purposes of creation. The fears or the folly of England prevented the bold experiment of excluding all idea of competition, by adopting the principle of common interest, founded on the enjoyment of common rights, and the desperate and barbarous alternative was embraced, of excluding competition by counteracting the tendencies of nature, by causing and continuing want and weakness, ignorance and disunion, and converting the powers of independence into instruments of servitude. Thus, the houseless peasantry and starving manufacturers of Ireland manned the fleets, and recruited the armies which enslaved her.

When England had established her free constitution, by the Revolution of 1688, and by seating the house of Hanover on the throne, when her commerce and her arms had enlarged her resources, and exalted her power above every other European state, her policy towards Ireland could be satisfied with nothing less than the positive and unequivocal expression of unbounded dominion over her. By the statute for better securing the dependency of Ireland upon the crown of Great Britain, an explicit and haughty declaration was made of the vile connexion between the master and the slave. The grave commentator on the laws of England was, by statute, authorized to initiate her youth in the pride of power, and the sophistry of ambition, and to store their minds in early life, when most susceptible of impressions for good or ill, with the unhallowed princi-

ples of oppression. By statute, the learned commentator
was authorized to select Ireland as an eminent illustration
of his doctrine, to enrol her specially in the pompous cata-
logue of countries subject to the crown of England, and to
tell her that, even previous to that statute, she was bound
by acts of the English parliament, whenever that parliament thought fit to include her under general words, or
particular nomination; and Ireland was instructed not only
in the law of her subjection, but in the reason of the law.
"It flowed from the very nature and constitution of a dependent state—dependence being very little else but an ob-
ligation to conform to the will or law of that superior person or state, upon which the inferior depends." She was
also informed of the original and true ground of this superiority, to which she was subject; and to which she was
required submissively to bow. "It was what is usually,
though somewhat improperly, called the right of conquest—
a right allowed by the law of nations, if not by that of
nature; but which, in reason and civil policy, can mean
nothing more than that, in order to put an end to hostilities,
a compact is either expressly or tacitly made between the
conqueror and the conquered, that if they will acknowledge
the victor for their master, he will treat them for the future as subjects and not as enemies."

When Molyneux denied that Ireland had been conquered by England—when he maintained the right of
Ireland to liberty by charters, and to independence by
her separate legislature, he only attempted to establish a
good cause by means unnecessary and fallacious. He
erred through an anxiety to fence his argument from every
possible attack. He erred through the vain expectation
that precedent might control those whom neither justice
could influence, nor pity melt; and that men who wielded the

sword of power, would respect the privileges of weakness,
because those privileges were not only matter of right but
of record. When Molyneux bowed "with the lowest
submission to the great council of England," he only be-
trayed the involuntary dejection of an honest mind uncon-
scious of its own humiliation. But, when the celebrated
commentator on the rights of Englishmen, who breathes a
pious prayer for their perpetuity, maintains that force
gives right, that Ireland was dependent by right of conquest, and by right of conquest was bound to obey the
laws which the conquerors should think fit to prescribe,
that the conquerors had a right to declare their own
opinion of their own title to plunder and oppress; and
when he lays down this doctrine with the solemnity of a
professor in an elaborate panegyric on law, and liberty,
and constitution, the friend of truth will enter his indignant protest against principles which reason and humanity
alike condemn, and will appeal from Blackstone and the
law of nations to the dictates of eternal justice, which man
too often violates, but never can change.

While an unprovoked invasion which involved Ireland
in centuries of darkness and blood was thus coolly and
deliberately advanced, and systematically taught by the
Vinerian professor to be the rightful origin of British rule,
while force, which she could not resist, was made a justification of the servitude to which she was consigned, the
condition of Ireland exhibited a dreadful exposition of the
avowed law of her dependence. The policy of depression
was carried to an extremity which seemed inconsistent
with the very selfishness from which it flowed. In the
year 1778, the wretchedness of Ireland appeared, for the
first time, to interest the British parliament. But it was
not the justice or the generosity of that parliament

which the wretchedness of Ireland had moved. It had excited meaner motives for relief. Individual members, in the zeal of party, or, perhaps, in the sincerity of virtue, might feel the force of the truths which they proclaimed, but the mass of that parliament was actuated by the cold maxims of prudence alone, in a wish to relax, in some degree, the commercial bondage under which Ireland pined. For some time, however, after this change in the temper of the English parliament, the people of England, less prudent than the parliament, could not perceive that even self-interest was deeply concerned in the demands of justice. Ireland was not only ruled by the temporizing policy of the English cabinet; she was also subject to the blind, ignorant, bigoted selfishness of the English manufactory, and English counting-house, which could not understand, or would not confess that Ireland might be sunk too low even upon the sordid calculations of commercial monopoly. The English minister yielded to prejudices, which, however marked by folly, or pregnant with mischief, he had not the virtue or the courage to withstand. The conduct which is not founded on the unbending principles of right, but on the pliant motives of expediency, is often reduced to the necessity of making severer sacrifices to fear than need have been made at first to justice. The parliament and people of England, by tardy and reluctant concession, were humbled to recantations which the haughty spirit of imperial rule could never have anticipated, and which it was scarcely possible could have been sincere.

The unfeeling and impolitic exercise of supreme legislation, on the part of England, terminated in the complete and absolute renunciation of the right to exercise it at all. Ireland was at length taught, by necessity, a lesson which she might long before have known from reason, and which she ought never to forget—she was taught to look to herself for justice, and to liberty for happiness. The effects of the memorable war between England and her colonies in North America will long be felt by the nations of Europe. England attempted to tax those colonies against their will, and England united and raised those colonies into a mighty nation. America triumphed, but the struggle between despotism and liberty was transferred from the new to the old world;—Europe was convulsed by the shock of antagonist principles. The contest is not yet decided, and the happiness or misery of ages may depend on the final issue of the conflict. From the era of the war between England and America, Ireland may be considered as acting, in some degree, by a distinct, separate individual impulse, contrasting her existence with that of England, and forcing herself upon the notice of the world, as a country which might, one day, be worthy to rank among independent nations. The power which had enslaved, impoverished, and insulted her, was reduced to the mortifying confession that she was unable to protect her. Ireland, thus abandoned and cast upon herself, in the exertions of self-preservation, disclosed the elements of greatness, as well as the means of safety. The important discussions to which the American war had given rise, and the glorious struggles of the American people for independence, had agitated, interested, enlightened, and elevated the Irish mind. The keen sense of appropriate suffering had produced a much stronger sensation than mere sympathy for the oppressed, or generous wishes for the success of a just cause. The Irish people had their own griefs—the inflictions of centuries, deep and direful—calling loud for redress or vengeance, compared to which the wrongs of which America complained were as nothing. Yet, America, when complaints were found to be unavailing, and remonstrance was treated with contempt, had set at defiance the fleets and armies of the wealthiest and most powerful nation in the world. The example was such as to make the slave aspiring, and the despot wise. The events which then took place in Ireland, excite mingled sensations of admiration and disappointment, exultation and sorrow.

The extreme distress to which Ireland had been reduced by a policy oppressive and improvident—the unexpected, extraordinary, and formidable change, from feeble lamentations to bold demands, and active retaliation, in a country which had so long languished in poverty, obscurity, and contempt—the awful sanction impressed on the laws of humanity and the rights of nature, by the formidable array of 60,000 volunteers in arms—the embarrassed situation of England, from a war, unjust in its principle, and, to her, disastrous in its events, at length demonstrated to the British minister the necessity of prompt and decisive concessions to Ireland. But it entered not into the imagination of that minister, that those concessions should extend beyond a relaxation of the excessive and absurd restrictions on the trade of Ireland, which had been rashly accumulated without regard even to obvious maxims of a prudential monopoly. The concessions proposed, as a relief for the distress, and a satisfaction of the complaints of Ireland, were entirely commercial. These concessions, though limited in their extent, and, in many respects, illusory in their operation, were important when contrasted with past commercial bondage, and might well justify the proud boast of a FREE TRADE. That there ought to be some relaxation of previous severity, seemed to be universally acknowledged. That such ample concessions were made, arose from the perplexity of fear and the temporizing spirit of expediency. While England possessed the supreme legislative power, those concessions might be modified, reduced, neutralized, or recalled, as future events and opportunities might render the change practicable or expedient. Perhaps, in the very moment of *liberality*, the British minister anticipated a season of less danger and greater arrogance, in which England might resume whatever portion of the concessions then made should be found formidable to her jealousy, or be felt humiliating to her pride.

But the pride of England was soon to experience much severer mortification. The spirit which had demanded and obtained for Ireland emancipation in trade, disdained to submit longer to the despotism which had reduced her to beggary and despair. The emancipation of the Irish parliament from the shackles of Poyning's law, and of Ireland from the dominion of the English parliament, seemed from experience absolutely necessary to the existence, and, in the delusive visions of enthusiasm, seemed all-sufficient to secure the independence and happiness of Ireland. The 6th Geo. I. c. 5, was repealed by an English act of parliament, the 22nd Geo. III. c. 52, and by a subsequent act of the English parliament—23rd Geo. III. c. 28, that parliament renounced *for ever* the right to bind Ireland by its laws, and declared and enacted "That the right claimed by the people of Ireland to be bound only by laws enacted by the king of England, and the parliament of Ireland, in all cases whatever, and to have all actions and suits at law, or in equity, which might be instituted in Ireland, decided in the king's courts therein, finally and without appeal from thence, should be, and was thereby declared to be, established and ascertained *for ever, and should at no time thereafter be questioned or questionable.*"

The lofty claims thus conceded were opposed, as long as they could be opposed with safety. The desperate counsels, which occasioned the loss of America, had been succeeded by more temper and more prudence, in a new administration; and the *apparent* complacency with which the claim of the English parliament to bind Ireland by its laws was finally relinquished, completed the satisfaction of a generous and confiding people.

But the humiliation of British pride was not the subversion of British power. The theory of despotism was changed; the despotism remained. That the crown of Ireland was an imperial crown, inseparably annexed to or united with the crown of Great Britain, or, in other more intelligible language, that the sovereign of England for the time being was therefore in that right to be sovereign of Ireland also, but that the kingdom of Ireland was to be a distinct kingdom, with her own parliament the sole legislature thereof, subject to a negative power in the crown; and that on this annexation and distinction, the interests and happiness of both countries were thenceforth essentially to depend, by the simple repeal of 1782, and the more explicit renunciation of 1783, constituted the delusive principle of Irish independence.

The power of forming and comprehending a complex abstract idea, cannot influence the investigation or determine the truth or falsehood of any alleged particular existence. The nature of the connexion between England and Ireland, at any given time, must depend on historical evidence, or actual personal experience, and not on the faculty of forming abstract ideas, or defining possible contingencies; and yet an acknowledgment of the compatibility of certain ideas, not conceded by the justice, but extorted from the fears of England, was supposed to anni-

E

hilate her ambition, her jealousy, the feelings and prejudices of ancient power, the inveterate habits of unrestrained
oppression, and the poignant recollections of pride chas-
tised. No, it may be said, this was not supposed, and
could not be expected. But, by the acquisition of her
own parliament, released from the fetters of Poyning's
law, and freed from foreign interference, Ireland obtained
security against the lust of power long indulged, and the
apprehensions of commercial jealousy—the ruling passion
of the British mind. Had Ireland, by her recent victory,
indeed obtained an independent parliament, the impossibility of being unjust might have imposed upon England
the necessity of being wise. But Ireland, in her
emancipated parliament, obtained not an *independent* legislature. That parliament had even at first opposed its own
elevation. Trained to provincial servitude, it seemed lost
to every sentiment of generous ambition. At length,
swept before an enthusiasm which it could not feel, but
dared not to resist, it participated in the triumph, and
then presumed to boast of glories which it was unworthy
to reflect.

Rome, in her decline, left Britain to herself—unable
longer to enslave or protect her.

In 1777, Britain, weakened and embarrassed by war
with America, France, and Spain, was obliged to confess
that, in case of foreign invasion, the government had not
troops to defend Ireland. There were, in fact, at the
time, scarcely 5,000 regular troops in the country. The
Volunteers arose. They were composed exclusively of
the gentry and middle classes of society, and were commanded by the then Earl of Charlemont and other Irish
noblemen of high rank and character. Their numbers
increased rapidly, and by some accounts are computed to

have amounted to nearly 100,000. To state that they amounted to 60,000 well-appointed and well-disciplined troops, cannot be considered exaggeration.

To defend Ireland against foreign invasion became unnecessary. To rescue Ireland from the political bondage under which she groaned, soon fixed the thoughts, elevated the hopes, and concentrated the energies of the Volunteers. Of that illustrious band, one stood forth pre-eminent beyond the rest. No calumnious breath can blight the honours that rest on Grattan's grave. His grave is in a foreign land—his grave is in the land of the oppressor, who enslaved his country, and still rivets the chains ; and that country will deserve the degradation which she endures, if ever she forgets the man who devoted the best years of his strength to her cause, and wasted the lamp of life in her defence. He strove for her independence with unshaken constancy to the last, with feeble body, but unbroken mind and unabated zeal. He strove in vain. The fortune of the patriot is glorious, even in defeat. Grattan has departed—but he has left to Ireland, for other and better times, an example of the dauntless spirit which makes tyrants tremble, and makes nations free.

The year 1782 is an era in the political existence of Ireland which must be remembered with pride, not because Ireland then ceased to be a province, but because Ireland then displayed the powers which mark her title to be a nation. In the victory of 1782 may be seen the strength of Ireland ; in the disasters which followed may be seen her weakness. Endeared by recollections, interesting to the feelings of a gallant, a warm-hearted, and a grateful people, the memory of the Volunteers of Ireland seems consecrated to eternal fame, but the faithful page of

history, which reflects their glory, must also transmit the
shadows which obscure it. "It was a sacred truth, and
written, as it were, in the tables of fate, that the Irish
Protestant never should be free until the Irish Catholic
ceased to be a slave." When the Volunteers, at Dungannon, declared that they held the right of private judgment
in matters of religion, to be equally sacred in others as in
themselves, when they expressed their joy in the relaxation of the penal laws against their Roman Catholic
fellow-subjects, and their opinion that it was a measure
fraught with the happiest consequences to the union and
prosperity of Irishmen, they uttered a sentiment more
honourable to themselves, and more interesting to their
country than any other contained in the important reso-
lutions of that celebrated assembly. Such sentiments,
proclaimed in a season of growing energy in the people,
when the resistless impulse of an hour might bear away
the prejudices of ages, seemed to announce the most
auspicious effects. But darkness still rested upon the fortunes of Ireland. The principle of action in the Volunteers was limited by its early objects. In the events of 1779,
1782, and 1783, their first hopes had centered, and their
best strength had perished. In those events were involved merely the emancipation of the trade and parliament
of Ireland; the trade, from extravagant restrictions—the
parliament, from Poyning's law and the direct supremacy
of the British legislature. The emancipation of Ireland
from British dominion was a distinct and more important
object, demanding new and more difficult exertions. Heated by the magnitude of their first efforts, the Volunteers
seem not to have timely perceived how very little complete success in those efforts might be connected with the
independence and happiness of their country. When

cooler reflection had succeeded to the ardour of victory, the real importance of the acquisition could be more distinctly ascertained. Reason soon discovered that much indeed remained to be done. But the spirit of enthusiasm had died, and unassisted reason was much too feeble for the contest. Whatever hopes may have been formed from the early liberality of the Dungannon meeting, they were soon dissipated. The extent of that liberality appeared to be bounded by a relaxation of positive penalties merely against the Roman Catholic. When, after the obtaining of repeal and renunciation, the Volunteers, seated in national convention, in the capital, announced to an anxious people their memorable plan for the reform of the Irish parliament, by which they would have excluded three-fourths of their countrymen from the rights of citizens, when they thus deliberately recorded their adoption of the same unjust and bigoted policy by which Ireland had been so long divided, weakened, and oppressed, from that moment their strength was gone, and their ruin inevitable. The very parliament which they had raised from obscurity and impotence to legislative power, might now insult them with impunity. In vain did some bold and liberal minds point out the only road to honour and to safety; in vain did late and magnanimous repentance attempt to repair the fatal error. The hour of triumph had passed away, and a period of long and disastrous mortification had commenced. The ruinous advice to desist from an attempt which might create disunion among the friends of reform of the Protestant sects, produced or increased the mischief which it affected to prevent, or professed to deprecate. Oppressed by their own dissensions on the question of Catholic emancipation, by their reverence for the opinion of men of undoubted integrity, but timid minds, or sectarian antipathies, who were adverse to that measure, by the artifices of the avowed or secret enemies of reform, who dreaded, in the union of Irishmen, the overthrow of a growing system of foreign influence, and domestic corruption—oppressed by the accumulated weight of the frauds and prejudices of ages; the Volunteers of Ireland gradually and finally sunk into the common mass of a deluded and ill-fated people.

The Volunteers were dismissed, with cold thanks for past services, and a supercilious recommendation to convert their swords into sickles, and their muskets into ploughshares—dismissed by that parliament to which they had given life and power, and the means of glory, and which, at no distant period, basely surrendered all, and erased the name of Ireland, as a nation, from the records of time.

A repeal of the act of the 6th Geo. I. c. 5., and a renunciation of any right or claim in the British parliament of legislating for Ireland, made by the 23rd Geo. III. c. 28, together with a repeal of Poyning's law, gave or restored to Ireland a distinct legislature, the sole acknowledged authority by which laws were afterwards to be made for Ireland, and exhibiting all the *forms* and *appearance* of an independent national legislature. But, while the parliament of Ireland, from the era of these boasted acquisitions, exhibited the form and *appearance* of independent legislation, that parliament remained essentially unaltered. It remained a dependent provincial assembly, neither representing the will, influenced by the feelings, nor identified with the interests of the Irish people. The acquisitions then made, however splendid in attainment, soon appeared to be important, only as they might be considered necessarily antecedent to a material and radical change in the composition of the House of Commons, one of the three estates in which the power of legislation was vested. According to the admirable theory of the British constitution, to which the Irish constitution, by the changes just mentioned, was supposed to be assimilated, the House of Commons ought to consist of a certain number of delegates, freely and frequently chosen by the people, and really and substantially representing the general will, so that no law should be made, or tax imposed, without the virtual consent of the nation. While a variety of opinions might be entertained as to the extent and form of the elective suffrage, and the duration of the delegated trust, best adapted to produce the desired effect; whether the right of suffrage should be universal or limited, and in what degree, and whether the renewal of the House of Commons should be annual, or triennial, or septennial, or at any other given period; there was no man who felt, or professed to feel, a regard for liberty, and an attachment to the British constitution who did not maintain or admit that, by the principles of both, the House of Commons ought faithfully to represent the collective body of the people, and be; at least, so constituted, that, though not chosen by all, it should be identified in interest with all; and should not be under the influence of sordid, personal, selfish motives, to betray the delegated trust. Reason demonstrated that on this faithful representation of the people, by the House of Commons, the distribution and balance of power in the constitution, and the secure and permanent enjoyment of every right which it conferred or guaranteed, must absolutely depend. Experience had confirmed the deductions of reason. The Revolution of 1688, in England, had practically illustrated and enforced the natural and indefeasible right in the people of forming a government agreeably to its own will; and of deposing governors, and new modelling the constitution. By that revolution, a solemn and important declaration was made of this right in the people, and new and stricter limits were assigned to the powers of the crown. But the representation of the people in the House of Commons was left untouched. That representation was quite inadequate to the acknowledged object of its action in the political system. After the Revolution of 1688, art was substituted for violence, corruption for prerogative; and the constantly increasing influence of the crown, from the period of that revolution, furnished strong and alarming evidence that the necessity of another revolution could only be averted by restoring or establishing that relation between the constituent and the representative, which, by making the House of Commons the faithful guardians of the people's rights, might secure liberty to the nation, and permanence to the throne. The sincere and provident friend of the constitution, devoted to liberty and fond of peace, saw, with deep concern, in the means of corruption and the progress of venality, the principles of that constitution gradually becoming but the vision of theory and the theme of declamation; and in the reform of its practical agency by its principles, saw the only road to safety. The greater the blessings of the liberty enjoyed by Englishmen, the more eminent the station to which their country had been raised by the superiority of its constitution, the greater ought naturally to be the anxiety to preserve sound and entire that part of the constitution from which its superiority evidently flowed; or, if become degenerate and corrupt, to restore it to health and vigour. Every right which that constitution was framed to confer or preserve, must be insecure, unless the people, by their representatives in parliament, should be the guardians of their own happiness.

The pre-eminence of the British Constitution rested on this foundation—on the government of the community by the general will, without the evils of democracy. The legislative powers of the crown and of the aristocracy could only be considered as wise and salutary checks, designed and fitted to secure the deliberate and real expression of the general will, by means of the Commons house, the proper organ of that will. In support of these principles, if authority be wanting, may be cited the authority of Blackstone—no heated, declamatory advocate of popular rights, but the cold, deliberate vindicator of the rights of conquest. Blackstone says :—

"The Commons consist of all such men of property in the kingdom, as have not seats in the House of Lords, every one of which has a voice in parliament, either personally, or by his representatives. *In a free state, every man, who is supposed a free agent, ought to be in some measure his own governor ;* and, therefore, a branch at least of the legislative power should reside *in the whole body of the people*. And this power, when the territories of the state are small, and its citizens easily known, should be exercised by the people in their aggregate or collective capacity, as was wisely ordained in the petty republics of Greece, and the first rudiments of the Roman state. But this will be highly inconvenient when the public territory is extended to any considerable degree, and the number of citizens is increased. In so large a state as ours, it is, therefore, very wisely contrived *that the people should do that by their representatives which it is impracticable to perform in person*—representatives chosen by a number of minute and separate districts wherein all the voters are, or easily may be, distinguished."

But while the theory of British liberty presented this fair and fascinating picture, it could not be denied that the very reverse of the picture was the true representation of the actual state of things. That while Englishmen exulted in Magna Charta, in trial by jury, in their bill of rights, in their habeas corpus act, in the sanctity of the "straw-built shed," which the king dared not violate, the preservation and continuance of all these blessings depended on a House of Commons notoriously corrupt, and under the influence of the crown. A conviction of the excellence of the principles, and the magnitude and danger of the abuses of the constitution, had impressed on the minds of wise and honest men in England, among whom might be counted also some of the highest rank and most splendid talents, a firm persuasion of the necessity of a reform in the representation of the people in the House of Commons there, as the salutary means of preserving liberty, without the shock and hazard of a revolution. And the attainment of this object, in the rapid progress of parliamentary corruption, gained daily new importance, and excited increasing solicitude.

While such was the state of public opinion in England, on the necessity of reform in its legislature, every general topic which could be urged in favour of the measure there, applied with tenfold force to the parliament of Ireland. But it was not general reasoning merely, however strong, derived from the principles of political liberty, and the glaring inadequacy of the existing representation of the people in the House of Commons there to give efficiency to those principles, which demonstrated the necessity of reform in that representation. A variety of appropriate causes belonged to Ireland, which identified reform with national existence—which presented it to the understandings and the feeling of an oppressed and impoverished people, not as the regeneration, but as the acquisition of a constitution, as the only means of emancipating their country from the bondage, and repairing the desolation and debasement of six hundred years. It required no proof from experience, to demonstrate that, constituted as the Irish parliament was, the late change in its political powers would only render it a more expensive instrument for administering British domination in Ireland, that the mode of ruling the province would be varied; but that, without a radical reform in the representation of the people, it must still remain a province, as before, dependent and degraded. What was the state of that representation? Out of three hundred members, of which the House of Commons consisted, the counties, counties of cities and towns, and the University of Dublin, returned but eighty-four, leaving two hundred and sixteen for boroughs and manors; and of this number of two hundred and sixteen, two hundred were returned by individuals, instead of bodies of electors; from forty to fifty of them were returned by ten persons; and with respect to the boroughs, several of them had no resident elector whatever, some of them but one, and on the whole two-thirds of the *representatives* of the people were returned by less than one hundred persons. Even the county representation—the only portion of this miserable system which, by any effort of the mind, could be conceived to express the popular will—was grossly defective in its principles, and corrupt in its practical agency. While the Irish House of Commons was thus composed, its slender connexion with the people by means of such of its members as could be called *elected,* was renewed but once in every eight years, unless accelerated by the royal prerogative of dissolution; even the election of this very small portion, which alone bore the semblance of representation, exhibited a disgraceful scene of bribery, intemperance, riot, animosity, and perjury.

The necessity of ruling Ireland through her own parliament, caused by recent events, made a seat in the House of Commons an object of keen and expensive contention to the crown and rival factions among the aristocracy. Every engine of intrigue, influence, and corruption was employed by the hostile parties; the peace of society was disturbed, the integrity of the elector awed or seduced, while a few rare instances of talent and patriotism returned to the parliament, served but to illustrate more strongly the baseness of the surrounding crowd, unmoved by the force of reason, the obligations of virtue, or the charms of eloquence, by the power of great example, or the dread of public scorn. To denominate a system, of which such a House of Commons constituted an essential part, on which the character and efficiency of the whole mainly depended, a free constitution, securing independence to Ireland, was an insult to the understanding, and a mockery of the wretchedness which had pined for ages under a foreign yoke. To look to such a House of Commons for the fruits of independent legislation; for protection to infant trade; for encouragement to industry, arts, science, and morals; for healing religious animosity by equal laws and impartial justice; for raising Ireland from a state of poverty and humiliation to prosperity, dignity, and strength; for guarding her rights and her interests from the force and fraud of foreign despotism, long enjoyed without control, and exercised without mercy; to look to such a House of Commons for virtue and energy like this, would be idle and absurd. Scarcely had the parliament been emancipated from the supremacy of the British legislature, when the question of reform in the Irish House of Commons began to engage the attention of the men by whose spirit and perseverance that emancipation had been effected. The necessity of such reform, in order to complete the work of *national emancipation*, forced itself with irresistible conviction upon every reflecting and unprejudiced mind, while the formidable array of a volunteer convention seemed calculated to bear down all opposition to the measure. In that convention, however, the ardour of generous enthusiasm had evaporated. In the demand of exclusive liberty for Protestants, that convention seemed to court the mortification which it suffered. By that fatal error, the support of Grattan, Ireland's best and wisest friend, was lost; and discord, her bane and her disgrace, obtained its usual triumph. History has seldom to record the conquests of reason over prejudice and passion. Her common and melancholy task is to track the footsteps of the warrior in blood and desolation; to exhibit the disastrous effects of false principle and malignant feeling—to connect the degradation of man with the causes of his weakness and corruption, and to detect and expose the profligate conspiracy of a few against the rights and happiness of millions.

When, upon the change effected in 1782, in the political condition of Ireland, a conviction of the necessity of a further change in that condition had been impressed upon the public mind; the very state of things which had produced that early and well-founded conviction began to operate its natural effect in creating a fierce and determined resistance to every attempt at reformation. The English minister had recovered from his perplexity and alarm, and had formed a fixed resolution, to oppose to the uttermost the increasing spirit of national emancipation, which could be satisfied and completed only by a radical reconstruction of

the Irish House of Commons; and the Irish parliament
furnished to the English minister the obvious means of op-
posing the spirit of national emancipation with success.
That parliament, by the change effected in its powers in
1782, had been raised to a rank in legislation, which was
found by experience to have bound more firmly together
the great majority of its members in a confederacy of private interest against the rights and interests of the public.
The force of foreign influence quickly succeeded to the force
of foreign legislation, and domestic corruption became
thenceforward the ready and effectual instrument of foreign
dominion.   The parliament of Ireland felt at once the advantage of its position, and, assuming to itself, as real cha-
racteristics, all the figurative epithets with which an ardent eloquence had emblazoned its recent exaltation, when
called upon to reform itself, arrogated the lofty tone of
offended majesty; dismissed the call with haughty defiance, and the volunteer convention bowed before the
idol which political superstition had clothed with omni-
potence.   The affected importance of national delegation,
by which no Roman Catholic was represented, served but
to render the humiliation of that convention more complete, from the consciousness that three-fourths of the
people uninterested in its success, could not sympathize in
its defeat. The Protestant mind, as yet disposed merely to
cease from persecution, but neither expanded to benevo-
lence nor enlightened to justice, was startled at the idea of
Roman Catholic liberty and equality of rights.   The Protestant convention felt its weakness, and retired from a
contest to which it was unequal; and the Volunteers of
Ireland experienced the first effects of *independent legislation* in the *constitutional* rebuke, that armed men should
not dare to overawe the parliament, by proposing measures

for its adoption at the point of the bayonet. This objection, adopted merely for the purpose of evasion, was studiously removed. The attempt was renewed, freed from the legal objection, and was supported by numerous petitions from all parts of the kingdom. William Pitt, son of the celebrated Lord Chatham, was then minister of England. His political career commenced with brilliant exertions in favour of parliamentary reform there. His lofty eloquence was mistaken for the emanation of an ardent and sincere mind. The cold duplicity of his character had not yet been unfolded. His advancement to power was considered as an era auspicious to liberty, and Ireland rejoiced in the commencement of an administration which effected the Union, and completed her annihilation. The second effort for reform met with the same determined opposition from the Irish parliament as the first. The partial murmurs of a disunited people were heard with indifference, and could be despised with impunity. The renewed attempt was founded on the same narrow basis of exclusive rights. As its principle was the same, so was its fate. It was rejected by the House of Commons, with marked contempt for the wishes even of that portion of the people to whose reiterated demands no objection could be raised on the ground of religious incapacity. In the variety of plans proposed for parliamentary reform, while particular objections were raised by parliament to each plan, it was reform itself, and not the particular plan, which really excited the opposition and caused the rejection. Every possible modification of reform would have been received by the Irish parliament and by the British minister with the same determined hostility. Reform in the House of Commons was, in fact, an attempt to subvert a system of monopoly and corruption in a venal and subservient aristocracy, by which that aris-

tocracy was made the pliant though expensive instrument
of British supremacy in Ireland.   After the direct legislative supremacy of the British parliament had been formally
abdicated and renounced, the dominion of England over
Ireland could only be maintained through an Irish parliament, really unconnected in sympathy and interest with the
great body of the people.   Hence, the opposition of the
British minister to reform in the Irish parliament originated in the same principle of ruling Ireland as a subject
state, by which she had been for ages desolated and oppressed.   And in the intestine divisions of Irishmen, foreign domination still found its ignoble but sure support.
This resistance to reform, on the part of the government,
was marked by acts of injustice and violence, which exposed
the vain imagination that, with the forms, had been also
transferred to Ireland the spirit of a free constitution.   In
attacks on the liberty of the press; in attempts to prevent
legal and peaceable meetings of the people, for the purpose of deliberating on the best means of parliamentary
reform; in proceedings by the summary and unconstitutional
mode of attachment against sheriffs for convening and
presiding at such meetings—proceedings subversive of the
trial by jury and a flagrant usurpation of power in the court
of King's Bench, in matters clearly out of its jurisdiction;
in these and other acts of licentious authority, was plainly
evinced a contempt for all acknowledged rights and privileges, whenever the violation of them seemed necessary or
expedient, in the views of the government, for repressing or
overawing the expression of public wishes or public dis-
content.   From the beginning of this conflict, the fixed
determination of the government to continue and defend
the system of ruling Ireland through the corruption of its
own parliament, at every hazard, may be clearly seen, and

ought to be distinctly marked, in order to form a just esti-
mate of the causes of the calamities which followed. In
the temper and conduct of the government, soon after the
triumph of 1782, and from thenceforward, may be seen
numerous instances of those arbitrary principles, that
haughty defiance of public opinion, and settled purpose of
subduing the rising spirit of the nation, which finally terminated in its destruction. While such was the obstinate
resistance opposed to parliamentary reform in Ireland, a
striking example was presented of the imperious necessity
of the measure, as the only means of guarding recent acquisitions and future hopes against foreign encroachment and
domestic treachery. The plan of a new commercial arrangement between England and Ireland, proposed by
the British minister in 1785, with all the circumstances
attending its progress and final issue, afforded a fine
illustration of the nature of those acquisitions, and the
foundation of those hopes. In the instance alluded to, if
no other proof existed, it was demonstrated, by an experiment addressed to vulgar capacity, that the security of
whatever Ireland had gained by repeal and renunciation,
and the prospect of any future good, depended altogether
on the attainment of such a reform in the representation of
the people, as would make the House of Commons really
guardians of the rights and interests of an independent
nation. Without such a reform, the destiny of Ireland
appeared evidently to rest on the mere will of the British
cabinet, and on the quantum of corruption which a British
minister might at any time find it prudent or necessary to employ for the easy administration of Irish affairs
—without such a reform, it was clear that the political and
commercial and financial views of British statesmen, that
the jealousy, the avarice, and the ignorance of the Bri-

F

tish merchant, and manufacturer, and mechanic, must
continue to be the rule of Irish freedom, and the stand-
ard of Irish prosperity. Have the foregoing pages given
an exaggerated picture of England's injustice, and Ireland's woes? Attend to the British minister himself.
In the commencement of this memorable transaction, he
confessed a truth which the wretchedness of ages had long
before proclaimed, "that the constant object of the policy
exercised by the English government, in regard to Ireland,
had been to debar Ireland from the enjoyment and use of
her own resources, and to make her completely subservient
to the interest and opulence of Britain, without suffering
her to share in the bounties of nature, in the industry of
her people, or making them contribute to the general interests and strength of the empire—a cruel and abominable
restraint, at once harsh and unjust, and as impolitic as it
was oppressive, as counteracting the kindness of Providence, and suspending the enterprize of man—that Ireland was shut out from every species of commerce, she
was restrained from sending the produce of her own soil to
foreign markets, and all correspondence with the colonies
of Britain was prohibited to her, so that she could not ob-
tain their commodities but through the medium of Britain
—that this was the system which had prevailed, and this
was the state of thraldom in which Ireland had been kept
ever since the Revolution." Within a very few years, indeed, according to the authority of the same minister, the
former system had been entirely reversed, and a liberal and
enlightened, and comprehensive policy had succeeded to
the jealousy and bigotry of past centuries. Upon this new
policy he now professed to act; with his mind irradiated by
this recent illumination, he brought forward his new system, " liberal, and beneficial, and permanent." But this

beneficent statesman, this eloquent advocate of Irish commerce and negro emancipation, had been led away by the romantic visions of speculative justice and theoretical humanity, and was soon *compelled* to acknowledge the necessity of adjusting his original plan, by the vulgar measure of British liberality. The original plan, in the form of eleven propositions, had been warmly received, and hastily adopted by the Irish parliament. But, notwithstanding this approbation of the Irish parliament, which seemed at first to have also pervaded the country at large, the proposed arrangement, however specious and alluring, was, in reality, a covered attack on the newly-redeemed rights of Ireland, in trade and constitution. The sagacity of a few had at once detected, and marked the deception. But it became unnecessary to impress, by argument, their conviction on the minds of others. The nation was soon roused from its dream of British generosity, by a direct attack, too plain to be disguised or mistaken. The eleven original propositions were returned to Ireland from the English parliament, enlarged to the number of twenty, so changed and modified, as to excite in a large portion even of the corrupt and unreformed Irish House of Commons, sentiments of horror and indignation, and some spirit of resistance. But, notwithstanding this partial demonstration of national feeling, these latter propositions, thus altered, containing a surrender of the lately-acquired *independence* of the Irish parliament in commercial laws and external legislation, together with a grant of perpetual tribute to England, and an abdication of Irish marine, these propositions thus injurious and insulting, thus restrictive of the infant trade, and mortal to the infant liberties of Ireland—these propositions, in less than three years after the lofty assertion by Ireland, and formal acknowledgment by

F 2

England of the national independence of Ireland, were supported by a prostitute majority of the Irish House of Commons, the supposed delegated guardians of that independence. But the propositions were abandoned by the British minister. At the commencement of his political career, he did not judge it wise to press a measure so justly odious to the Irish nation, when he found that the spirit which had awed Britain in 1785 was not yet altogether extinct. The corruption, however, of the parliament, which in 1785 could surrender the glories of 1782, might well inspire him with the hope that, at some future and no very distant period, a more fatal attack might be attempted with success upon the separate and new-born existence of Ireland, and, without deserving much credit for sagacity or foresight, he might anticipate in a parliament, thus vile and traitorous within three years after its deliverance from bondage, the consummation of its baseness at the close of the eighteenth century.

Though the measure embodied in the commercial propositions was abandoned by the British minister, it was in its nature and circumstances calculated to awaken serious alarm in the people of Ireland, for the safety of that trade and constitution from which so much national prosperity was fondly expected.

The measure had *professedly* been brought forward by the British minister, from a conviction on his part of the justice and expediency of a more equal and liberal arrangement of the commercial intercourse between England and Ireland. From that *free* trade which, in 1779, had been granted by the policy, or extorted from the fears of England, Ireland had derived few of those benefits, respecting which such sanguine expectations were at first indulged. With all her boasted attainments of commerce and inde-

:pendence, her manufacturers were starving. Protecting
:duties on certain articles of merchandize were loudly called
--for by the people, and sternly denied by the Irish parliament, not on any principles taught by Adam Smith, but
-under the more convincing influence of William Pitt. The
idea of an Irish parliament protecting Irish trade by enact-
ments hostile to British monopoly, presented an appearance of practical national self-management wholly incompatible with the British policy of imperial regulation. That
policy could only be satisfied by compelling the Irish
people to look from their own legislature to England for
relief from commercial thraldom.

The original plan of the British minister, as contained
in his eleven original propositions, was viewed by the most
-sagacious and best informed with distrust, as illusory in its
-proffered benefits, and insidious in its compensations.
But, admitting it to be as liberal and beneficial as its ad-
-vocates proclaimed, it soon appeared that Ireland must
depend, not on the comprehensive wisdom and justice of
the statesman, but on the narrow bigotry of the counting-
-house. If the minister was, indeed, sincere in his frank
confession of past wrongs, and solemn profession of future
amendment, he soon repented of his rash integrity. He
quickly learned that to sacrifice the interests, invade the
-rights, and despise the sufferings of Ireland, were settled
traditional dogmas of British policy in trade, which he
must hold sacred and act upon steadily, if he wished to
continue prime minister of England. Accordingly, his in-
genuous candour and munificent liberality terminated in an
attempt to take advantage of the dejection of an impoverished people, and to cheat them into a surrender of both
trade and legislation; and a majority of the Irish House of
Commons was found base enough to conspire with foreign

perfidy against the independence of their country. When within three years after repeal and renunciation—within three years after England had abjured all claim to imperial legislation, and had solemnly recognized the absolute and unlimited right of the Irish parliament to legislate exclusively for Ireland, such an attempt could be made by a British minister, and be supported by an Irish House of Commons, all abstract reasoning on the necessity of reform in that body became superfluous. An example pregnant with melancholy instruction, was now addressed to the common sense and common feelings of every Irishman, who could reflect or feel on the rights and interests of his country. Uniformly plundered and oppressed by England, and almost blotted out from the knowledge or memory of other nations, Ireland, in a moment of resplendent glory, had redeemed herself from obscurity and reproach. But her difficulties seemed to multiply with her pretensions. The claim of independence was a claim to danger as well as to happiness. The danger seemed every day to increase, the chances of happiness seemed every day to diminish. The Irish parliament advanced in confidence as it advanced in corruption. Neither emanating from the nation, nor sympathizing in the national distress, it contemned the sentiments, and sacrificed the interests of the people. Not only the great measure of reform in the representation of the people, but, with perfect consistency, every attempt at subordinate reform was resisted by that parliament with haughty defiance, or dismissed with insulting contempt. A place bill, a pension bill, a responsibility bill, were successively rejected by large majorities in the House of Commons; and with circumstances of such marked indifference to the opinion, the grievances, and the complaints of the people, as not only demonstrated the

magnitude of corruption, but evinced the desperate purpose of defending it to the last, under every form, and in all
its excesses. The corruption was even audaciously avowed
by the servants of the crown in the *representative* assembly
of the nation. Peerages were sold by the government, to
purchase seats in the Commons; and all inquiry into this
monstrous abuse of the royal prerogative was refused.
The infamous traffic of boroughs was carried on with shame-
less publicity. Private jobs for the aggrandizement of particular families or individuals were either originated in the
parliament, or received its sanction. A system of profligate
expense was supported by a system of profligate taxation,
injurious to the industry, the health, and the morals of the
people. A mean aristocracy, courted, flattered, paid and
despised, calumniating the country which it oppressed,
reviling the wretchedness which it plundered, had convert-
ed the new legislative powers of the Irish parliament into
a source of private revenue. The nation, taxed without
its consent, paid the bribes by which it was undone, and
England raised a tribute in Ireland by means of an Irish
parliament, to perpetuate the old relation of imperial rule,
and provincial subjection under the new phraseology introduced at the era of 1782.

In the course of a very few years from that memorable
era, the anticipations of reason had been fully confirmed
by the evidence of experience. A reform in the national
representation, which political sagacity had immediately
connected with the important events of that period as in-
dispensable to Irish independence, was a measure soon
brought home to the understandings of ordinary men by
personal observation of existing circumstances; and a
strong conviction of its necessity had easily pervaded the
uncorrupted, by far the largest portion, of the community.

The foreign power which had roused resistance by an assumption of direct supremacy in legislation, enforced with senseless severity in matters of trade, still continued, through the medium of corruption, an indirect and injurious domination. That domination, exercised with more temper as to commerce, but with the same disregard of the political rights and interests of Ireland that such domination had ever displayed, by what it vouchsafed to grant disclosed more clearly the benefits withheld. Even the security of any commercial advantages conceded to Ireland depended upon interested fluctuating views of commercial policy in England. On her own parliament, Ireland could have no reliance ; and, if happiness consists not only in the actual possession of good, but also in the expectation of its continuance—if the enjoyment of present bliss cannot be perfect without excluding all distressing apprehension of future interruption—it was impossible that Ireland, with such a parliament, could ever feel the joys of possession, or the pleasures of hope; One page only, in her history of six hundred years, could furnish the pleasures of memory.

While a recent advancement of Ireland in trade was admitted, it was observed to bear no proportion to her capacities, and the amelioration of the wretched state of the lower orders of the people seemed not to be in the least degree promoted by the change. The same squalid poverty, the same debasing ignorance, the same vices and the same crimes—the offspring of that poverty and that ignorance, continued to exhibit unequivocal symptoms of deep and untouched defects in the constitution, or in the administration of the government by which their destiny was controlled. The wretchedness of the lower orders of the people in Ireland depended upon a variety of causes, constituting in the aggregate that miserable system by which this country had been ruled for centuries of desolation, and which nothing but a radical change in the principles of legislation and finance, and in the entire political economy of the state, could ever effectually remove. Such a change could be expected only from a parliament really national, which, identified in interest with the rest of the community, would consider the comfort and morality of the great mass of the people the chief object of its care, as the chief end of its institution: While the lower orders of the people could be sensible only of their misery, but could neither discern the cause nor comprehend the remedy, it was felt and acknowledged by every enlightened person in the country not interested in perpetuating abuse, and the opinion had deeply impressed all the middle classes of society, that from parliamentary reform alone could be expected any great and permanent good. But while the national feeling in favour of the measure was general and ardent, the minds of those friends of reform who could most influence and best direct public opinion, had been much agitated and divided as to the nature and extent of the reform which ought to be insisted on as necessary and safe. This difference of judgment in the friends of reform among the Protestant sects, arose chiefly on the question—whether the Roman Catholic should be comprehended equally with the Protestant, in the proposed improvement of the representation of the people in the House of Commons. This was a question, above all others, calculated to engage the most violent passions, the most obstinate prejudices, and the most lively apprehensions of the Protestant mind. Protestants, in general, had been for some time advancing towards the idea of emancipating Roman Catholics from

the severe and impolitic penalties and prohibitions of the
Popery code, but the idea of granting to the Roman Catholic a full and complete participation with the Protestant,
in all civil and political rights, was violently opposed by a
number of Protestants, honest and enlightened, and whose
attachment to the cause of liberty and their country could
not be doubted, but whose reasonings had taken a bias from
their prejudices and their fears, too powerful to be changed
by argument or experience. The opinion that to admit
the Roman Catholics to a community of civil and political rights with Protestants, would endanger the established religion, and the then settlement of property in
Ireland, had hitherto prevailed. It was an opinion which
the first great advocates for parliamentary reform either
actually entertained, or to which they submitted, from a
belief that that measure could be more easily carried unen-
cumbered by Roman Catholic claims, and that, under a
reformed Protestant government, at no very distant period,
all distinctions, grounded on mere religious sectarian
differences, might, with safety, be abolished. The experiment of obtaining *exclusive* reform, however, had been
made, supported by men of great talent, by some of high
rank, and still higher character, and, above all, supported
by the authority, the weight, and the pressure of an
armed association, formidable in fame, in numbers, and
in property. The experiment had been made, and failed;
and the decided and high-toned defiance with which the
attempt was received, by the House of Commons, seemed
to astonish and confound the delegated organs of such
various and commanding titles to respect. The experiment of *exclusive* reform was again made under other
auspices, and again failed. It was opposed by a combination of circumstances too powerful to be over-

come by the partial efforts of a divided people. While the evil and the remedy agitated all passions, and were canvassed by all understandings, the cause of defeat became every day more apparent, and the necessity of calling forth the energies of all, clearly proved the injustice of exclusion.

In tracing the subjection and the calamities of Ireland, from the first introduction of the English power down to the formal abdication, by England, of her legislative supremacy in 1783, the disunion of Irishmen must appear to every attentive observer to have been the chief cause of their defeats and degradation. This disunion originally invited invasion, and made conquest permanent. At different intervals, the power of the invaders was shaken. But the want of general views and co-operation among the natives terminated in the common subjection of all. When every attempt to expel the invaders from the country was finally relinquished in despair—when a vast portion of the inhabitants had been rooted out by the sword, or by legal proscription, and the space which they had occupied had been filled up by Englishmen—when the descendants of the early colonists had become Irishmen in interests, in feelings, and in sufferings, it might seem reasonable to expect that the connexion by which the two countries were placed under a common sovereign, would become a connexion of reciprocal advantage and equal rights, and that Ireland, in her usefulness and strength, would possess the guarantee of prosperity and independence. Such, indeed, might have been the final issue of things in Ireland, but for the unfortunate circumstances by which the disunion of Irishmen was prolonged in a new and more disastrous form. But the ultimate division of

the Irish people into two great religious denominations
enfeebled both, and delivered them up an easy prey to the
power which oppressed them, infatuated instruments of
their mutual ruin. Religious bigotry blinded alike the
Protestant and the Roman Catholic, destroyed or blunted
the social and kind affections, engendered cruel and inveterate suspicions, and the personal experience of the ex-
sting generation was borne down by the hereditary antipathies of the preceding. At the era of the volunteers, these
religious antipathies had become less violent, and in the
progressive liberality of that illustrious body might have
for ever perished. But the growing sentiment of general
liberty was checked by the artifices of the interested, the
violence of the intolerant, the apprehensions of the timid,
but, above all, by the authority of some men of revered
worth, and deserved influence, who, from prejudice or
from prudence, were decidedly adverse to the admission of
Roman Catholics to an equality of political rights with their
Protestant countrymen. Before the error was fully understood and felt in all its effects, the early ardour which
might have repaired the mischief had ceased. It became
necessary to kindle a fresh spirit, proportioned to the
objects to be attained, and the difficulties to be encoun-
tered. The magnitude of the abuses to be reformed, the
obstinacy with which those abuses were defended, the
discomfiture of past exertions, the increasing danger of
delay, seemed to demand new and extraordinary efforts.

To emancipate public opinion from destructive prejudices, to cleanse the Protestant character from the stain
of persecution, to exalt the Roman Catholic from mental
thraldom and political debasement, to turn all parties from
the bitter remembrance of past hostility, and from mutual

crimination, to the consideration of a common country, oppressed and impoverished through the miserable delusion of its people, to dissolve the artificial and mischievous connexion between politics and religion, to substitute national enthusiasm for sectarian zeal, to unite all hearts, and combine all talents in the pursuit of parliamentary reform, by interesting the entire people in its attainment, and, by means of a legislature really independent, to secure to Ireland the free exercise of her own powers, and the full enjoyment of her own resources, presented to the bene-volent, the generous, the ardent, the bold, and the aspiring spirit, the noblest objects of ambition—not the ambition which destroys, but the ambition which saves—not the ambition which exults in the guilty conquests of the sword, but the ambition which glories in the pure and im-mortal triumphs of the mind.

Those objects were not attained. The eighteenth century closed, and Ireland was found in deeper darkness, sorrow, and humiliation by far, than when, in 1782, for the first time during a period of six hundred years, a bright ray of joy and hope cheered the dreariness of her existence. The parliament which, in 1782, had been lifted to the power of becoming great and beneficent, in 1800 sunk into the lowest depth of self-debasement. In 1800 was passed the Act of Union, declaring and enacting that, "the King-doms of Great Britain and Ireland should upon the first day of January which should be in the year 1801, and for ever, be united into one kingdom, by the name of the 'United Kingdom of Great Britain and Ireland.'" One would think that the ancient poet saw, in prophetic vision, the base and prostitute portion of Irishmen who voted for that union, when, in describing the Tartarian regions, and their inhabitants, he places conspicuous amongst them the wretch who sold his country for gold:—

> " Vendidit hic auro patriam dominumque potentem
> Imposuit : fixit leges pretio atque refixit."

From that union what has followed? Ireland restless, because not free : England feared and hated—the tyrant's wish—*oderint dum metuant.*

But has Ireland now a right to have that act of union repealed? An undoubted right. It was passed by a body of men delegated merely to make laws for the internal government, and the administration of the internal affairs of Ireland, and the conducting of her external trade and relations with other countries, but without any right or authority whatsoever to destroy, change, or alter the fundamental principles of the constitution, and of its own existence.

The Act of Union was, on the part of the Irish parliament, considered in the abstract, and without any reference whatever to the means by which that parliament was wrought upon and moved, a flagrant and iniquitous breach of trust, rendering any compact with England—a party to the breach of trust, for effectuating that union—absolutely null and void against the Irish people, according to every principle of natural law and political justice. When there is added to this the gross and indisputable corruption by which the Irish parliament was bribed to violate the trust, and pass the Act of Union, where can exist a doubt of the right of the Irish people to have that act repealed?

But how is this right to be enforced—how is this repeal to be effected? Ay, there's the rub. Is repeal to be effected by force—by physical force—by force of arms? No. The attempt would be vain, and wicked because it would be vain. Ireland is not able to stand alone. Then repeal must be effected by MORAL FORCE—that mighty principle, which makes princes patriotic, statesmen sentimental, and imperial parliaments just and philanthropic—which softens the hearts of gaolers, opens the doors of prisons, and sets the captive free. " But previously I should have mentioned the very impolite behaviour of Mr. Burchell, who, during this discourse, sat with his face turned to the fire, and at the conclusion of every sentence would cry out *fudge*, an expression which displeased us all, and in some measure damped the rising spirit of the conversation."

Monster meetings—a hundred thousand full-grown Irish peasants, with bones matured, and well clothed in muscle, accustomed to cold, and hunger, and toil, to whom a good row would be a luxury, and fighting a recreation; these things were no mental abstractions, but plain, intelligible, common-sense, practical, embodied existences, not physical force in actual operation, but clearly intended and clearly understood to be physical force for threat and intimidation. The threat might be idle, and the hope of intimidation vain—despised by the statesman, and laughed at by the soldier, but the meaning and the object of monster meetings, and the speeches made at monster meetings, were not to be mistaken; there was no deception, no chicanery in them; they were employed for intimidation, or they were employed for nothing; they were employed by men, (will those men deny it ?) endowed with wisdom to gain a noble object by terror rather than by the sword, but gifted with courage to use the sword, if terror failed. Not cold-blooded cowards, who would whet the weapon they were afraid to wield. Demonstration of great physical force, for the purpose of intimidation, and thereby obtaining changes in the constitution, may not be *vocabula artis*, may not be a tech-

nical description of any offence indictable by law, but to
any person but a fool or a lawyer—to common men, with
common minds, the meaning of the words, as applicable to
monster meetings, is obvious and impressive.

But what is moral force? The moral-force men have
not defined it,—and, in dealing with complex ideas, unless
we define the terms used to express them, we may dispute
for ever. Of moral force, then, until a better description
be given, let the following be taken. Moral force is a
power, by the mere operation of reason, to convince the
understandings and satisfy the consciences of those on
whom the effect is to be wrought, that there is some particular moral act within their ability to perform, which
ought to be performed, and which it is their duty to perform; and also, by the operation of the same divine principle only, making those free moral agents do the very
thing required. The intended effect must be produced,
and must be moral—the efficient cause must be moral,
purely moral, unmixed, unadultered by any mean or sordid views; reason, heavenly reason, applied with eloquence
divine; no threat, no intimidation, no cold iron, no " vile
guns," no " villainous saltpetre digged out of the bowels
of the harmless earth," nought but the radiant illuminations
of moral truth.

In this intellectual process there is a circumstance, however, well worthy of reflection for the philosophical mind,
as something out of the common course of mere mental,
spiritual operations. It is this, that money, which used
in former times to be considered and called the sinews
of war, of physical force, not in demonstration or poten-
tially merely, but in actuality, in re, in esse, in sabre
cuts, and bayonet thrusts, and gun-shot wounds, became
the sinews of moral force also, insomuch that it was quite

apparent that if the Commons should refuse to grant the supplies for carrying on the moral war, there would be an end of it, showing a striking analogy in this respect, at least, between spiritual and material causality.

After this change had been effected, this magic change from monster meetings, and inflammatory speeches, from athletic peasants, broad shoulders, and brawny muscles, high sounding words and chivalrous defiance into moral sentiment and soft-persuasion; when no voice but the still, small voice of conscience was to be heard; when all material instrumentality, pitchforks, and pikes were sublimated into pure spiritual agency; when every clodpole was to philosophize, and become a Socrates or a Paley; when moral force was to be the sure and only pledge of national peace, national wealth, national plenty, national strength, and national independence, swaying all men of all minds, and women too, save only, and always excepted, French princes and Spanish infantas. When this strange, and sudden, and romantic transformation had taken place, then, forthwith, repeal of the Union became not only a lawful, but a harmless cry — no longer striking the hearts of English statesmen with fear and tribulation, but, on the contrary, bringing with it confidence and joy. Forthwith free discussion, free opinion, and free expression of opinion upon repeal of the Union, became the evaporation apparatus of relief from the high and dangerous pressure of the grievances, the calamities, the sufferings, and the complaints of Ireland. This evaporation apparatus was most kindly and opportunely furnished by the moral-force men; the expediency statesmen gladly availed themselves of the happy contrivance, and began immediately to apply it. This new policy, the work of master minds, commenced by the restoration of

G

justices of the peace, who had been dismissed as avowed repealers, to their former magisterial dignity, with an express or implied license to cry out "Repeal of the Union" as lustily as they could and pleased; and the longer and louder the cry, the greater of course would be the quantum of evaporation and relief from the pressure which threatened the new administrators of Irish affairs with difficulty and danger. Epistles replete with liberal, constitutional doctrine, on the one hand, and with grateful acknowledgment and complimentary diction on the other hand—all quite worthy of the first place in the next edition of the "Complete Letter-Writer," examples of statesman-like compositions being much wanting in former editions—passed on this memorable occasion. The repealers were astonished, relieved, and enlightened, and could not well complain that even-handed justice should extend the same liberality to Orangemen as to them. In truth, the evapo-ration plan, like great talents, was of universal applica-tion. This *novum organum scientiæ* for the government of Ireland, though not marked by the genius of a Bacon, seemed to be considered by the expediency-men of the day as a first-rate contrivance. Our friend Burchell might, perhaps, interpose with his impolite damper, and cry, "Fudge!" But Burchell was not a man of the world. He was a plain, downright country gentleman—a real gentleman—a man of integrity and honour, who never said one thing and meant another; he was not a prime minister—he knew nothing of puff, humbug, or bamboozle —nothing of political effect, or state manœuvre, or tem-porary expediency—nothing of the secret springs by which great minds are moved; and, therefore, although all this evaporation apparatus of moral force and eloquence be-stowed upon it, restored magistrates and touching epistles,

" The larum bells of love" might, to a blunt man like Burchell, appear mere hum. It may fairly be said, Burchell is no authority in such matters. *Communis usus facit jus—*

> "Of all trades and arts, in repute, or oppression,
> Humbugging is held the most ancient profession,
> 'Twixt nations and parties, and state politicians,
> Prim shop-keepers, jobbers, smooth lawyers, physicians,
> Of worth and of wisdom the trial and test
> Is, mark ye, my friends—who shall humbug the best."

But, without entering critically into this inquiry, will the present minister say—will any friend or adviser of the minister say—will any man, who has gained place or profit by recent ministerial changes, say—will any man of common sense and common honour say, that it is really intended, or desired, or expected by the minister, that the moral-force action for a Repeal of the Union, with all its vaunted power, will have the slightest effect in obtaining it? Is not the minister decidedly hostile to the measure? What is to make him change? Is the moral force to work the miracle? Within what time? The argument in favour of a Repeal of the Union is as easily made, and as easily understood in an hour as in a thousand years. If not long since fully understood and duly appreciated by the minister, on this subject eternal dulness must be his portion. But, if fully understood and duly appreciated by him, what will he do respecting it? Will he propose a Repeal of the Union of Great Britain and Ireland in the imperial parliament himself, and advise her majesty to recommend the consideration of the measure by parliament, in her next speech from the throne? or will he support the measure, if brought forward and proposed by others? or will he leave it an open question? or will

he oppose and resist the measure, with all the force
of his talents, and all the weight of his influence, as a
measure unjust, unwise, and ruinous to the prosperity,
the happiness, the strength, and the safety of the British
empire?   If the moral-force repealers are honest and
sincere, if their moral-force principle be not, indeed, a
mere instrument of faction and finance, fit only for mys-
tagogues to live by, exhibiting their relics and collecting
their pence, if they, indeed, possess moral courage—the
only courage of which man should boast, for animal courage he has in common with the brute—if their speeches
for Repeal be not mere noisy, ostentatious, vapouring,
good-for-nothing vauntings, or worse, fraudulent con-
trivances for self-aggrandizement and popular deception,
to be repeated and prolonged, while a single penny
can be wrung from unsuspecting confidence, blind credu-
lity, or suffering poverty, to gratify mean avarice or heart-
less ambition, let a Repeal of the Union be sought and
demanded, and nobly fought for, as a people's right, in
the imperial parliament, where only moral-force men, upon
their own principles, can seek redress.   Unless Repeal of
the Union, by moral-force men, be a perfect political
asymptote, always approaching but never to reach the goal;
unless it be planned and intended to be such, deliberately
and fraudulently, and as such is licensed by the government, like some of these other deleterious exciseable commodities by which British domination in Ireland has been
strengthened, and the Irish people have been impoverished,
and besotted, and inflamed; unless such be, indeed, the
scandalous conspiracy between moral-force men and the
British minister, to beguile, to dupe, and to betray a gallant
and confiding race; let that minister be bearded at once
with the question—is he a friend, or is he an enemy to a

CPSIA information can be obtained at www.ICGtesting.com
Printed in the USA
LVOW111923010113

313900LV00006BA/413/P